Zest for Life

by

Diane Clement

Foreword by Umberto Menghi

RAINCOAST BOOKS

Vancouver

First published in 2000 by

Raincoast Books
8680 Cambie Street
Vancouver, B.C.
V6P 6M9
(604)323•7100

www.raincoast.com

1 2 3 4 5 6 7 8 9 10

CANADIAN CATALOGUING IN PUBLICATION DATA

Clement, Diane, 1936-
Zest for life
Includes index.

ISBN 1-55192-292-4

1. Cookery. I. Title.
TX715.C5774 2000   641.5   C00-910027-X

Cover design: Gabriele Chaykowski
Interior design: Ruth Linka

THE CANADA COUNCIL | LE CONSEIL DES ARTS
FOR THE ARTS | DU CANADA
SINCE 1957 | DEPUIS 1957

Raincoast Books gratefully acknowledges the support of the Government of Canada, through the Book Publishing Industry Development Program, the Canada Council for the Arts and the Department of Canadian Heritage. We also acknowledge the assistance of the Province of British Columbia, through the British Columbia Arts Council.

Printed in Hong Kong

To my family
Doug, Jennifer, Rand, Suzanne and Vincent,
and to our Clement and Matheson clans,
with endless love

Contents

From left: Me, my friend Gloria Smith and Umberto Menghi taking time from Umberto's Villa Delia cooking school. What fun we all had with Umberto as we toured the famous "Saturday markets" in the heart of Tuscany.

Foreword

I'VE MET WITH DIANE CLEMENT ON MANY OCCASIONS. Most recently, she was a guest chef at my cooking school in Tuscany. Her energy and her love for mingling food and people had always scared and impressed me, but the ten days we spent together in Tuscany turned out to be one of my most memorable times there. Her fresh, crisp, colourful and healthy, organized confusion in and around the kitchen was delightful and amusing.

Whether Diane is at the Tomato Café in Vancouver or preparing the ultimate macaroni and cheese at the cooking school in Italy, she continues to show us her championship approach to cuisine and living. It takes courage for a Canadian to come to Italy to cook the ultimate macaroni and cheese – that's like carrying coal to Newcastle – but I was really impressed. Her captivating and colourful storytelling held everyone's attention and both Diane and the macaroni came through smooth and creamy.

Upon occasion, Diane and I have discussed what makes people get up in the morning, full of energy, ready to face the day whatever it may bring. Repeatedly, her answer to me has been: Life is fun – try and share it with others. Diane thrives on this basic principle and she practices it very well in her own life.

Leafing through this book, I was struck by how it gathers all that Diane is committed to and holds dear: family, friends, food and adventure. It's a walk down memory lane with restaurants on both sides. *Zest for Life* is a true reflection of her philosophy of living and enjoying life. Like me, Diane Clement is a great believer that you are what you eat.

– Umberto Menghi

Introduction

WHILE GROWING UP IN THE MARITIMES, IN MONCTON, NEW BRUNSWICK, LITTLE DID I envision the impact that sports would have on my life. Becoming an international athlete and part of the Canadian Olympic team would offer me the unique opportunity to travel the world, and those experiences would ultimately lead to my love affair with ethnic foods and diverse cultures as well as my pursuit of a healthy lifestyle.

My life in sports began in 1952 when my dad and other track and field enthusiasts founded the Moncton Olympic Club. I began training in the 100- and 200-metre sprint events, which were the only running events for women at that time. (It wasn't until 1984, at the Los Angeles Olympic Games, that the first marathon for women was held. It was won by an American woman, Joan Benoit.) So I trained for those two events, and in 1954, while competing in Toronto at the Canadian National Exhibition (CNE) as part of the Canadian Olympic Training Programme, I broke the 100- and 200-metre records to become a double Canadian champion.

In 1955, my family moved to Montreal, where I enrolled at Sir George Williams University and joined the Mount Royal Athletic Club. My goal was to participate in the 1956 Olympic Games to be held in Melbourne, Australia. Much to my delight, I made the Canadian Olympic team in the 100-metre and 200-metre sprints as well as the 4x100-metre relay. Years later, in 1979, I was honoured to be inducted into the New Brunswick Sports Hall of Fame for my participation in the Olympics.

What an exciting and overwhelming experience it was to travel to Melbourne and meet and compete with world-class athletes in a truly global village. All of us had one thing in common: a strong will to compete and to be the best we could be in our particular events. But we also had the opportunity to enjoy our diverse cultures and different cuisines, sharing with one another in the Olympic dining room.

Melbourne not only marked the beginning of my passion for world cultures and cuisine, it was also where I met Doug, the love of my life. Doug had represented Canada in the 1952 Olympics in Helsinki, Finland, in the 400- and 800-metre events, and in Melbourne he was the captain of our Canadian track and field team. Although we both retired from competition in 1958 following the Commonwealth Games in Cardiff, Wales (my greatest thrill was winning the bronze medal in the 4x100-metre relay there), the two of us have been "on the run" ever since!

In more recent years, Doug and I have been active in presenting lifestyle lectures at conventions, on British Columbia Automobile Association (BCAA) cruises, and at athletic seminars around the world. Wherever we travel, we usually start the morning with a leisurely jog exploring the particular town or city we're in. We take note on our runs of the small, family-operated restaurants, or ones we have read about, to visit later that day or evening. On our return to Vancouver, I always attempt to re-create our favourite memorable dishes for our family and friends.

My travels have given me so many special opportunities to meet and cook with chefs from around the world who share the same passion for food as I do, and I've learned so much from them. They've been mentors who have encouraged me to continue teaching cooking classes over the past three decades, and they've also inspired me to write four Canadian best-selling *Chef on the Run* series cookbooks, and my fifth Canadian best-selling cookbook, *Diane Clement at the Tomato*.

My ultimate joy, however, was the opening of the Tomato Fresh Food Café in 1991 with my daughter, Jennifer, and former partners Jamie Norris and Haik Gharibians. In 1995, we welcomed a new partner and general manager, Christian Gaudreault. The Tomato Café continues to grow and succeed with our energetic team of Jennifer, Christian and me at the helm.

As I reminisce over the past five decades, I think about the tremendous explosion of global cuisine that has occurred. As with any fashion, what is hot one year is passé the next, but the classics never fade away. From the comfort foods of the fifties and sixties, to the international cuisine of the seventies made easy with the help from an icon like Julia Child, to the artsy, sparse *nouvelle cuisine* of the eighties, to the "towering" *haute cuisine* of the nineties, we've seen it all!

As we enter the 21st century, the food trends are once again focussing on comfort foods, or contemporary home cooking. From the ethnic foods of the Mediterranean, Africa, South America and the Pacific Rim to the diverse cuisine of North America, today's chefs of the world are seeking only the best of fresh ingredients for their dishes, which are simply presented, nourishing and memorable. Ask any successful chef, "Who did you learn the most from?", and in most cases the response will be, "My mother and grandmother, watching them do their magic in our kitchen, taking the simplest ingredients without the state-of-the-art kitchen and equipment, and creating a masterpiece."

For me, too, my fondest memories of food are of my mom's simple home cooking prepared with such ease. My older brother Joel, my twin brother David, Dad and I were spoiled by Mom's ingenuity and natural ability to make any simple dish a scrumptious affair, whether it was Friday "fish night," often with tasty fish cakes or a hearty seafood chowder, or a special anniversary or birthday dinner of chicken à la king in patty shells and jellied anything. And, of course, the most requested family Saturday night casserole was Mom's unbelievable macaroni and cheese. In the nineties, this casserole is as popular as ever with some of the top restaurants in North America still featuring it on their menus. In fact, it always sells out at the Tomato Café whenever we have it on our special chef's plate for lunch or dinner. I've updated Mom's original recipe by making it a three-cheese dish and adding Dijon mustard.

Sunday dinner was also a time that we all looked forward to, not only to catch up on all our week's activities, but also to enjoy Mom's special surprise menu. As Mom would bring in the main dish, I would announce its arrival with an off-tune blast from my tuba, which I played in our Moncton High School Band. Needless to say, my career playing the tuba (as well as the bass violin) was short lived! Doug and I carry on the family tradition of Sunday dinners whenever we can. My 92-year-old dad often attends and treats us with his tales of the early years. It's also a time for me to present the old classics, along with my latest new recipe to surprise our family and friends.

The best compliment any cook can receive is the smiles of loved ones as they tuck into each course, with the buzz of great conversations around the table. Over the past five decades, it has been times such as these, shared with family and close friends over a warm, comforting meal, that have given me so much "zest for life." The past 45 years of involvement in both the world of international sport and global cuisine has been an inspirational journey that I happily share with my family, friends, chefs and athletes from around the world. Now, I am delighted to share my zest for life with you.

Relaxing after a workout with my Olympic family from around the world at the 1956 Olympic Games in Melbourne, Australia. From left: Barbel Mayer of Germany, Gunhild Larking of Sweden, Fleur Mellon of Australia, Hermina Geyser of South Africa, me, Kate Delbarre of France, Francisca Sanopal of the Philippines, Amelia Wershoven of the United States and Dana Zatopekova of Czechoslovakia.

How To Use This Book

IN CREATING THIS COOKBOOK, IT WAS IMPORTANT BOTH TO ME AND THE PUBLISHERS that we present recipes that were tasty, healthy and accessible. To make the recipes of the past five decades as user-friendly as possible, each one contains a **preparation time** and many include a **less fat** alternative and a special **Diane's secret** technique or tip. Here is how to best use these friendly cookbook features:

Preparation time: I don't know what your kitchen looks like the night before a dinner party when you're "cooking up a storm," but I can tell you mine looks like a tornado just blew by! My kitchen is small, and I always have several dishes going at once. Pots and pans, bowls, dishes, casseroles, cooking utensils and recipe ingredients are everywhere. I also like to leave the drawers and cupboards open, so I can get at everything quicker, and I hate cleaning the dishes as I go. Whenever Doug is around, he takes over "sink duties" which joyfully speeds up my preparation. I figure it's quicker to clean up one big mess than several small ones when time is of the essence. Consequently, the preparation times I mention – which do not factor in the time it takes to actually cook, bake or chill the dishes, just the time it takes for "prep work" – are approximate, depending on the number of dishes you may decide to do at once!

Less fat: Many of the recipes of the fifties, sixties and seventies were high in fat. By the eighties and nineties, we were all becoming more health conscious as we tried to balance diet and exercise. For many recipes, I provide some quick tips and alternatives for cutting down the fat content. In some cases, however, for special entertaining, I have left the recipes unchanged (e.g., Cheese Fondue, page 14). Changing the cheese ingredients would completely alter the taste and texture of this particular dish. We can have our special treats from time to time, we just can't do it every day.

Diane's secrets: Having made most of the recipes in *Zest for Life* tons of times over the past five decades, I know most of them backward and forward. For many, I have provided a few tricks of the trade that make the difference between a dish's success or failure. I also give advice on how to present a dish and where to find a particular ingredient that may be foreign to you. I hope my little secrets will be of assistance! It feels a little like "coaching" you from the sidelines!

Many of the dishes in the photos are deliberately shown exactly as you would create them in your own kitchens and not as "food art." What a challenge it was for me to prepare over 30 food shots with talented food photographer John Sherlock. It was a three-day marathon! John, and his assistant Alastair Bird, would dash from my kitchen to our patio to photograph the food as I produced each dish.

Thank heaven the weather cooperated! Carol Watterson, Associate Publisher of Raincoast Books, was my lifesaver, assisting me in the kitchen, dashing off to the store for more ingredients and cleaning up after me. I couldn't have prepared so many dishes without her. The remainder of the dishes were shot at the Tomato Fresh Food Café. There were no touch-ups to the photos in this book – what you see is what you get: it's all real, tasty food! Enjoy!

The Fabulous Fifties

Drinks

SAN FRANCISCO'S FAMOUS RAMOS GIN FIZZ   12
SPANISH SANGRIA   13

Appetizers

APRÈS-SKI CHEESE FONDUE   14
CANADIANA SCALLOPED OYSTERS   16

Salads

THE GREAT CARUSO'S CRAB LOUIS   18
DOUG'S FAVOURITE SALAD DELUXE   20
SHIMMERING ORANGE MANDARIN JELLIED SALAD   21

The Fabulous Fifties and Sixties

Doug and I were married in May 1959, the week after he graduated from the University of British Columbia Faculty of Medicine. We headed for San Francisco, where Doug was to commence his internship, in our 1938 Plymouth.

Before settling for the year in San Francisco, we decided to travel to Acapulco, Mexico for our honeymoon. We purchased a '52 Oldsmobile and loaded it with a case of Campbell's Cream of Mushroom soup, a case of canned tuna, several boxes of instant rice, six giant jars of peanut butter, jam and crackers and a large electric fry pan we received as a wedding gift. A "gourmet" honeymoon it was not!

I must admit, we were extremely naive about the rugged travel in Mexico at that time. It was an adventure we'll never forget. It was a rough world out there on the many unpaved roads to Acapulco. We spotted villagers in the mountains wearing grass capes and carrying machetes, we saw dead cattle and dogs on the roadside, and we experienced rainstorms that blinded us while driving through the mountain ranges on narrow, dark, winding roads. We also experienced a fire in our trunk from heat combustion as we were driving.

On that trip, we came to the conclusion that if we survived our honeymoon, we could survive anything. For months after our adventure, we couldn't look at canned mushroom soup, tuna or instant rice! But in spite of all the surprises, we kept our sense of humour and had a lot of fun. On our 40th anniversary in May 1999, in Madrid, Spain, we drank a toast to the many world adventures that came to follow our challenging Mexican honeymoon.

Our return to San Francisco after our honeymoon marked the beginning of the California Dreaming era. Casual entertaining was the "in thing," and the other interns at Doug's hospital and their wives would have parties on the weekends with chuck steaks marinated for hours then thrown on the barbecue. The original Caesar salad, which is believed to have originated in southern California in the early 1920s, was a "must" along with potatoes Romanoff and lots of Christian Brothers' wine. Blum's Coffee-Toffee pie was the ultimate grand finale. It was informal entertaining at its finest, and so fond are my memories of these casual get-togethers, that I just had to include recipes for Steak Superb, California-Style (page 40), Potatoes Romanoff (page 24) and Blum's Coffee-Toffee Pie (page 60) in this chapter.

At that time, cookbooks were few and far between. My favourites were *The Joy of Cooking,* first printed in 1931 and known as "the encyclopedia of cooking know-how," Mom's Maritime cookbooks and *Fannie Farmer's Boston Cooking-School Cook Book,* first printed in 1924. As well, *The Foods of the World* from the Time-Life cookbook series were a great source of the history of the cuisines of the world. *Larousse Gastronomique,* first published in France in 1938 but not published in the United States until 1961, with all its legendary tales and recipes, has been my bible on the origins of foods. The great Georges Auguste d'Escoffier wrote the preface for the first edition but died before it was published.

The first cookbook that Doug gave me was the *Better Homes and Gardens Cookbook,* which I still refer to often. In fact, I've used it so much, it's falling apart.

One of the most unusual pocket book cookbooks I picked up in San Francisco in the late fifties was *Playboy's International Gourmet.* I'll never forget its cover, which promised, "You can prepare exotic meals easily with special color photos of foreign fare." The menus included items such as The 20-minute French Gourmet and The English Hunt Breakfast. Believe it or not, the recipes were sensational, and the book became an international bestseller.

Cooking magazines were also starting to surface at the time, and *Gourmet, Sunset* and *Bon Appetit* were the babies of the food magazine explosion. Every amateur cook rushed to the magazine stands to seek the hottest recipes of the month. As well, "professional" chefs were keen to see what chef was featured and what dishes they had presented.

Our year in San Francisco gave me the opportunity to take in many cooking classes and introductory wine seminars. We would treat ourselves once a month to a special restaurant that we had read about or that had been recommended to us. The San Francisco restaurants were, and remain, among the best in the world. It was a culinary year for us, dining out in a city known for its spectacular views and cable cars appearing over the rolling hills in the heart of the city. Best of all was tasting the fresh abundance of seafood at restaurants overlooking the water and enjoying the robust California wines from the nearby booming wineries. Today, we return often to San Francisco to try new restaurants and to recapture the exciting times we had many years before in one of the most beautiful cities in the world.

When we moved back to Vancouver in 1960, Doug joined the general practice of Dr. Dick Talmey and Dr. John Varley in Richmond, B.C. At that time, Richmond was a small rural community with 25,000 people and many of the local farms offered an abundance of fresh vegetables and summer berries. Richmond now boasts a population of over 125,000, with only a few of the original farms still producing fresh produce.

In the early sixties, we were busy raising our children, Jennifer and Rand, and starting a local track and field club, the Richmond Kajaks. Consequently, dinners were usually "on the go" featuring the children's favourite spaghetti sauce, the old faithful Kraft's macaroni and cheese, and many casseroles, usually tuna or chicken! Yes, those canned soups and fish casseroles were our standbys, and I couldn't resist including recipes for Ruth Matheson's Nova Scotia Seafood

Casserole (page 44) and Jennifer and Rand's Tuna Noodle Casserole (page 38) in this chapter!

The fifties and sixties were a time when the most outrageous appetizers appeared in magazines and cookbooks. Even back then, in the early days of entertaining, we all had our "what's hot and what's not" list. Looking back, there were quite a few appetizers of the "what's not" variety – apple slices as the base for nippy cheese balls, pineapple slices with a mound of creamed pineapple cheese on top, and cubes of Cheddar cheese on a Ritz cracker topped with a pretzel stick! These were a few of the "gourmet" appetizers appearing in the original Better Homes and Garden Cookbook and magazines of the time. We had the nerve to call this "the happy hour"? No wonder "Scotch on the rocks" was the number one drink at the time! Anything to kill the taste of those morsels! Needless to say, these openers didn't become classics! 🙴

In the mid-sixties, Barbara Watts invited me to do a cooking session at the new YWCA in Vancouver. The class followed a fitness class, the first ever for both in Vancouver. The trend toward a healthy lifestyle with more focus on diet was just beginning and exploded over the next three decades.

Entertaining at home was also becoming more popular. Seven of my friends invited me to join them in a gourmet luncheon group to meet every month or so. We eventually became known as The Gourmet 8. We met eight times a year for lunch, with the hostess and her co-hostess presenting a luncheon menu with recipes from around the world.

Then in 1969, we decided to take the best of our luncheon menus and publish them in a cookbook called, naturally, *The Gourmet 8*. The book sold for $3.75 and it was such a success we published a second book in 1974. The two books were the first cookbooks of that nature to be published in Vancouver.

Next, we were approached by a major publishing company to do a national cookbook. We turned the offer down because of all our busy schedules, but we still experienced our group's success through another channel. We had sold many of our books in Calgary, and a few bridge players who had served some of our recipes at their get-togethers came up with the idea to do their own book, *The Best of Bridge* – and the rest is history!

Thirty years later, The Gourmet 8 now consists of seven, and we still meet for our luncheons and continue to present fabulous recipes.

The late sixties was definitely the beginning of home cooks becoming more adventuresome in their entertaining and in their everyday cooking for their families. Local grocery stores were introducing gourmet sections with many import products being introduced. Mind you, these "global" selections didn't include much more than canned Belgium carrots, French mustards, Scottish Duck consommé and Russian caviar, but it was the beginning of more to come. We had a limited selection of greens to choose from, with iceberg lettuce, spinach, romaine and watercress being the main options. And the popular wine of the night was the Spanish Mateus Rosé or Faisca.

Fondue parties were going strong, and the classic Spanish Paella (page 46) and Sangria (page 13) were the hit of summer parties. We in The Gourmet 8 realized that one of the most pleasurable events was a great dinner party at home with our friends and family. And when I look back at our gourmet group and our two cookbooks, I am amazed at how creative we were. Even today, people tell us, "You know, I still enjoy those recipes from your cookbooks."

So, in tribute to the fifties and sixties, here are some of my all-time favourite classics. Some I've updated to reflect the change in today's eating habits. Many of the recipes included in this chapter were, back in the fifties and sixties, rich and high in fat content. Those have been modified without sacrificing taste. Others I've left unchanged. As Anne Murray sings in one of her songs: "anything old is new again." Four decades later we are seeing some of these old classics appearing on restaurant menus to rave reviews.

I hope these recipes from the fifties and sixties will bring smiles to the faces of your friends and family and that you will raise your glasses to toast your moms and grandmothers who prepared their simple comfort foods with love and passion. Enjoy!

SAN FRANCISCO'S FAMOUS RAMOS GIN FIZZ

SERVES 6

This was the rave "brunch" drink during the fifties and sixties at all the San Francisco area restaurants. It's a gin drink with cream, eggs, citrus fruit and cracked ice – a sophisticated milkshake! We never did find out where the name came from, but we assumed a bartender in San Francisco, named Ramos, created this landmark drink.

Try this creamy concoction at your next brunch; it's smooth and sensual! I like to serve this drink in wine or martini glasses.

INGREDIENTS
6 oz gin or vodka
½ cup fresh lemon juice
¼ cup fresh orange juice
4 tsp sugar, or more to taste
4 large eggs
1 cup whipping cream
Few dashes orange flower water (optional)
2 cups crushed ice
Fresh mint
6 thin slices orange for garnish

METHOD
Mix all ingredients except the ice, mint and orange slices in a blender until creamy. Refrigerate until just before serving. Add crushed ice, swirl again in blender, pour into glasses, and garnish with mint and oranges.

PREPARATION TIME: 10 minutes

 DIANE'S SECRETS *Orange flower water can be obtained in the specialty sections of some supermarkets or health food stores.*

SPANISH SANGRIA

Like the matador and his bull, every paella must have its sangria! With the Spanish influence so strong in San Francisco, some of the best dinner parties back in the fifties and sixties would star the traditional paella (see my recipe for Spanish Paella, page 46), along with a well-chilled sangria. At your next Castilian dinner party, invite a flamenco dancer and a guitarist and your guests will be shouting "olé!"

INGREDIENTS
1 large orange
¼ cup granulated sugar
2 cups fresh orange juice
1 26-oz bottle dry red wine
½ cup orange-flavoured liqueur (e.g., Cointreau, Grand Marnier, Triple Sec)
2 oranges, peeled and sliced
1 large apple, sliced
2 lemons or limes, sliced
2 fresh peaches or nectarines, sliced (optional)
Ice cubes
Club soda

METHOD
Several hours before serving, use a vegetable peeler to thinly cut off the outer peel or zest of half the orange. In a bowl, rub the sugar over the peel with your hands to release the flavourful oils. Add orange juice, red wine and liqueur. Cover and chill for 15 minutes, then remove the orange peel and add the fruit. Chill until serving.

Serve in a punch bowl or pitcher, adding to each glass a few pieces of fruit, some ice cubes and a squirt of soda.

PREPARATION TIME: 10 minutes

DIANE'S SECRETS
It's best to make sangria early in the day, or at least three to four hours before serving for the fruit flavours to peak. I usually use a good red wine with a light fruity flavour, such as a Beaujolais or a Gamay. The Spanish Rioja is excellent as well.

APRÈS-SKI CHEESE FONDUE

SERVES 6 TO 8

In March 1999, the Canadian Academy of Sports Medicine held its annual meeting at Whistler, one of the top ski resorts in the world. One of the events for the conference was evening snowshoeing on a lighted course, followed by a sensational fondue party at Joel's restaurant at the Whistler North Golf Club. I was awarded a Whistler sweatshirt for devouring the most cheese fondue! We can't eat cheese fondue every day, but on special occasions, like a fun snowshoeing evening, it's awesome. ๕

Back in the fifties and sixties, I think every bride received a cheese and beef fondue set as a wedding gift. (I was given six!) Consequently, everyone had fondue parties. They were a quick and easy way to entertain. The outstanding Swiss-invented cheese fondue is a big hit around the world – so much so, that four decades later fondue parties are still high on the list for après-ski get-togethers. For entertaining your friends, I suggest making this cheese fondue as a meal on its own, with plenty of salad, complemented with your own wine choices, beer or a mulled wine. For other excellent fondue meal ideas, see The Fondue Party (page 50).

INGREDIENTS
1 large clove garlic
2 cups dry white wine
1 lb imported Gruyère or Emmentaler cheese,
  or a blend of both
3 tbsp flour
Pinch pepper
Pinch nutmeg
6 tbsp kirsch or 6 additional tbsp wine
2 loaves French bread, cut in 1-inch cubes
  (crust on each)

METHOD

Peel the garlic and rub it over the bottom of a chafing dish or any 2-quart flameproof enameled casserole. Pour in the wine and heat slowly.

Toss together the cheese and flour. When the wine starts to bubble, add the cheese mixture in small handfuls to the pot, stirring with a fork until the cheese is melted before adding another handful. When the fondue is smooth and starts to bubble, add the pepper and nutmeg. Slowly pour in the kirsch or extra wine and blend well. Keep the sauce warm over a candle or burner.

To serve, put the cubed bread in a big basket alongside the fondue pot. Spear the bread with a fondue fork, going through the soft part first and securing the points in the crust. This way you are less likely to lose the bread.

PREPARATION TIME: 30 minutes

(You can grate the cheese, cube the bread and measure the other ingredients ahead of time and be all set to go at the last minute.)

Less fat: What can you do to this fondue classic to cut down on the fat content? It's a special treat, so enjoy it once or twice a year, and don't over-indulge!

DIANE'S SECRETS

If the fondue becomes too thick, pour in a little warm white wine and blend.
Have plenty of extra bread on hand.

CANADIANA SCALLOPED OYSTERS

This oyster dish is a classic! From the shores of the Maritimes, to the west coast of Vancouver Island, this is truly a Canadian dish. It's been our longtime family tradition for holiday entertaining or for those times when we've been able to dig our own succulent oysters. Even those who claim they hate oysters keep coming back for more.

INGREDIENTS
1 quart fresh shucked oysters in their juices
   (available at local fish markets)
½ cup butter
½ cup flour
1 tsp Hungarian or other sweet paprika
1 small onion, finely chopped
1 large clove garlic, crushed
½ green or red pepper, finely chopped
1 tsp Worcestershire sauce
1 tsp lemon juice
Pepper
½ cup cracker crumbs

METHOD

Cut oysters in small pieces and cook in a medium-size pot for about 4 minutes in their own juices. Set aside.

In a heavy skillet, melt the butter, add flour and stir until well blended and light brown. Add the paprika, onion, garlic and green or red pepper and cook for about 4 minutes. Remove from heat and add Worcestershire sauce, lemon juice, oysters and their juice and a good dash of pepper. Mix gently, pour into a shallow baking dish that can be taken to the table. Sprinkle with cracker crumbs. This recipe can be prepared to this point and refrigerated for up to 24 hours.

To serve, bake at 375°F for about 30 to 40 minutes, or until hot and bubbly. Serve with thinly sliced rye or sourdough bread, cut in small cocktail-sized wedges.

PREPARATION TIME: 20 minutes

Less fat: Cut down the butter by 2 tbsp, which won't affect the texture.

THE GREAT CARUSO'S CRAB LOUIS

Numerous Crab Louis recipes have been in circulation since its origin. Basically, the original Crab Louis salad included fresh crab (never use canned, frozen or artificial), hard boiled eggs, iceberg lettuce and tomatoes, topped with a tart chili sauce mayonnaise dressing. The original recipe called for whipped cream, but I use sour cream in my recipe instead. Fresh shrimp, as well, can be substituted nicely, or try the combination of fresh crab and shrimp. This is my version of an old Seattle and San Francisco classic.

INGREDIENTS
1 lb fresh crabmeat
2 cups celery, thinly sliced on the diagonal
1 head iceberg lettuce, sliced in thin julienne strips
3 ripe avocados, peeled, seeded and cut in half
3 large hard-cooked eggs, cut in quarters,
3 small tomatoes, cut in 6 wedges
1 lemon, cut in 6 wedges

DRESSING
2 cups mayonnaise
½ cup sour cream
½ cup Heinz chili sauce
¼ cup green onions, finely chopped
¼ cup fresh parsley, finely chopped
1 tsp Dijon mustard
2 tbsp lemon juice
1 tsp Worcestershire sauce
2 drops Tabasco
Pinch each of pepper and salt

Back in the fifties, the Crab Louis salad was made famous at the Palace Hotel in San Francisco, opened in 1875 and one of the world's grandest hotels at the time. However, the story goes that this salad actually originated in Seattle, Washington. Apparently, the great opera singer, Enrico Caruso, was appearing in Seattle when a chef by the name of Louis served a crab salad to Mr. Caruso after his concert. Caruso then asked Chef Louis for his recipe because he couldn't stop eating it. Sometime later the Crab Louis salad surfaced on the menu at the Palace Hotel's majestic Garden Court restaurant. How it got there we'll never know, but it became the most popular salad in San Francisco. I'd like to think that if Enrico Caruso had a taste of my version of this salad today, he would shout "Bravo! May I please have more?"

METHOD

Blend all dressing ingredients together in a bowl. Store in the refrigerator for up to 3 days.

For the salad, combine the crab and celery in a mixing bowl with about ¼ cup of the dressing, or just enough to bind. Divide the lettuce among 6 salad plates, placing some in the centre of each plate. Place one half an avocado on top of the lettuce. Spoon the crabmeat mixture into the cavities of the avocado halves. Alternate wedges of eggs and tomatoes, two each per plate, around avocado. Garnish with a lemon wedge on each plate.

PREPARATION TIME: 15 minutes

Less fat: Use low-fat mayonnaise and sour cream, and just coat the crab with the dressing.

DIANE'S SECRETS
Be sure to use Heinz chili sauce; other brands have a totally different chili component.

DOUG'S FAVOURITE BACON, LETTUCE AND PEAS SALAD DELUXE

SERVES 8

Loads of bacon, mayonnaise, cheese, peas, onions, iceberg lettuce all layered, then tossed at the last minute made this decadent salad a hit in the sixties – as it is today. In fact, when we shot the photos of the food for this book, we all had fun sampling the many dishes, and Salad Deluxe was a winner: one mouthful and you're hooked! For our Father's Day family dinner, I always make Doug's all-time favourites, and this salad is a must. Try it with barbecued chicken or steak. It's wild!

Less fat: Reduce slightly the amount of mayonnaise, cheese and bacon OR substitute low-fat mayonnaise and cheese, and cut down on the bacon or use none at all. This is a rich salad, so you need small helpings only. Use it for special celebrations!

INGREDIENTS

3 to 4 heads of lettuce, cleaned, dried, broken
　　into medium-size pieces
1 cup mayonnaise
1 sweet white onion, thinly sliced
Sugar
Salt
Pepper
1½ cups green peas, slightly cooked
1 cup Swiss cheese, sliced in thin julienne strips
½ lb bacon, crisply fried and crumbled

METHOD

Early in the day of serving: Reserve a bit of the lettuce and a few dots of mayonnaise for the topping. In a tall, clear-glass salad bowl, layer a third of the remaining lettuce and dot with several spoonfuls of remaining mayonnaise. Top with a third of the onion slices, sprinkle with sugar (about 1 tsp on every layer) and add a dash of salt and pepper. Add a third of the peas, cheese and bacon in an even layer. Repeat layers 2 times, ending with reserved lettuce and mayonnaise. Cover with plastic wrap to seal well and refrigerate. Do not toss. Just before serving, toss gently and serve immediately.

PREPARATION TIME: 20 minutes
(While the peas are being cooked and the bacon crisped, slice the cheese and onions and break the lettuce. Now you're ready to layer the salad!)

SHIMMERING ORANGE MANDARIN
JELLIED SALAD

The "queens" of salads in the fifties and sixties were the jellied creations adorning every buffet. We had at least four or five fancy jelly moulds to show off our latest recipes, from tomato aspic to fruit jelly. This orange combination ranked number one! It's colourful, tangy and full of shimmering mandarin oranges. Children adore this salad. Even today, it would be a big hit as a complement to a buffet, especially one featuring baked ham and scalloped potatoes. So search out those old jelly moulds and throw in a little nostalgia for your next family buffet dinner.

INGREDIENTS
2 packages (4-oz size) orange jelly powder
1½ cups boiling water
1 can (12-oz size) Minute Maid orange juice
   concentrate, undiluted
2 cans (10-oz size) mandarin oranges, drained,
   saving juices
⅔ cup mandarin orange juice

METHOD
Dissolve jelly powder in boiling water, add orange juice and stir well until blended. Add mandarin oranges and juice. Pour into an oiled mould and refrigerate overnight. Remove from mould and serve on lettuce greens decorated with sliced oranges.

PREPARATION TIME: 10 minutes

MARITIME CLAM OR SEAFOOD CHOWDER

SERVES 6

Friday was always "fish day" at our home in Moncton, New Brunswick, and one of my fondest memories is of Mom's hearty clam or seafood chowder. We preferred the Maritime or New England style, unlike the Manhattan style with tomatoes added. Mom would often add some white fish, such as halibut or cod, to the basic clam chowder. If you use clams only, try adding an extra cup of clams to make up for the fish.

Serve this chowder with Grandmother's Tea Biscuits or Scones (page 54), with Cheddar cheese added for a savoury touch!

INGREDIENTS
4 slices bacon, or ¼ lb salt pork, cut into small cubes
1 small onion, chopped
5 medium potatoes, peeled and cubed
3 tbsp green pepper, chopped (optional)
2 stalks celery, chopped
2 carrots, chopped
1 clove garlic, crushed
2 cups chicken stock
1 tsp Worcestershire sauce
Salt and pepper to taste
3 cups raw baby clams with juice or 2 cans
    (14-oz size) baby clams with juice
1½ lbs halibut or cod, cut in 1-inch cubes
2 cups light cream

METHOD

In a large, heavy saucepan sauté the bacon or pork until crisp. Add onion, potatoes, green pepper, celery, carrots and garlic, and sauté for about 2 minutes more. Add chicken stock, Worcestershire sauce, salt and pepper. Cover saucepan and simmer for about 15 minutes, or until potatoes are tender. Mash the mixture slightly with potato masher.

In a separate pan, heat clams in their juice for about 3 minutes and add to the vegetables. Simmer the fish in 1 cup of water for about 4 minutes. Add both fish and water to the saucepan. Stir in the light cream. Refrigerate until ready to serve, then reheat until hot.

PREPARATION TIME: 45 minutes

Less fat: Use less bacon or salt pork, or none at all. Substitute skim milk for the cream. Always skim off any fat layer that may settle on the top of the soup in the pot.

DIANE'S SECRETS

If the soup becomes too thick when reheating, add a little milk to thin it to the desired consistency.

POTATOES ROMANOFF

This potato dish has been around since the early fifties and continues to appear at family get-togethers and informal buffets. It's great for summertime barbecues! It can be made a day ahead and reheated before serving. The original recipe called for Cheddar cheese, but I like to combine two or more cheeses.

Less fat: Cut down on the cheeses, or use low-fat cheese. Use low-fat sour cream.

INGREDIENTS
6 large baking potatoes, such as Idaho
⅓ cup chopped green onions
Salt and pepper to taste
1½ cups cheese, divided (Cheddar, Parmesan, chèvre or a combination)
2 cups sour cream

METHOD
A day ahead or morning of serving: Peel and cook the potatoes just until tender. Cool and grate into a large bowl. Add the onions, salt, pepper and 1 cup cheese and fold in the sour cream. Put into an 8½ x 11-inch casserole and cover with the remaining cheese.

Refrigerate until ready to bake. Take out of fridge 1 hour before baking.

Bake at 350°F for about 35 to 40 minutes or until golden and hot.

PREPARATION TIME: 30 minutes

DIANNE'S CARROTS AU GRATIN

SERVES 12 TO 14

Dianne Matheson, my sister-in-law who lives in Toronto, made this dish for Doug and me in the sixties and it's still one of our family favourites in the nineties. Marvellous with roast chicken, turkey and pork. The longer it bakes, the tastier it becomes!

Less fat: Use low-fat cream cheese.

INGREDIENTS
8 oz Philadelphia solid cream cheese
1 can (10-oz can) cream of celery soup, undiluted
½ cup milk
Salt and pepper to taste
3 lb carrots, grated
1 cup bread crumbs
4 tbsp melted butter
½ cup sharp Cheddar or Parmesan cheese, grated

METHOD
Butter a shallow 1-quart casserole. Combine the cream cheese, soup, milk, salt and pepper in a blender or food processor until blended. Add carrots and blend well. Pour mixture into the casserole.

Mix the bread crumbs, melted butter and cheese and sprinkle on top. Cover and refrigerate overnight.

Bake uncovered at 350°F for 45 to 50 minutes, or until golden and bubbly. If the topping becomes too brown, cover with aluminum foil.

PREPARATION TIME: 15 minutes

GARLIC MASHED POTATOES

SERVES 6

An absolute hit with all lovers of mashed potatoes, this dish also makes a wonderful accompaniment to meat loaf (see Old-Fashioned Meat Loaf, page 34). The garlic adds a new twist to this simple fifties side-dish classic. If you're a turnip fan, add mashed turnips to the mashed potatoes before adding the butter and milk.

INGREDIENTS
8 large potatoes, peeled and quartered
5 or 6 cloves garlic, or to taste, peeled
   and sliced in half
Salt to taste
1 medium turnip, peeled and diced (optional)
3 tbsp butter
Milk or light cream, or combination
Pepper to taste

METHOD

Put the potatoes, garlic and salt in a large pot and cover with boiling water. Simmer until the potatoes and garlic are both tender. Drain well and mash. If adding the turnip, cook separately in a pot of boiling, salted water until tender. Mash and add to the potatoes. Add butter and milk, and fluff to the desired creamy consistency. Add salt and pepper to taste.

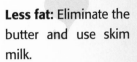

Less fat: Eliminate the butter and use skim milk.

For an extra garlic punch, mash 4 or 5 roasted cloves of garlic and add to the mashed potatoes. To roast garlic: Toss with a little olive oil. Wrap in tinfoil and bake at 375°F for 30 to 40 minutes or until softened and golden.

PREPARATION TIME: 35 minutes

DIANE'S SECRETS

For special occasions such as Christmas dinner, I hate to prepare the potatoes at the last minute. I always make them a day ahead, and reheat them in the oven. My mom had a secret to keeping them fluffy, and not tasting reheated a day later: Whisk egg yolks with a little milk and add to the mashed potatoes. I use 1 yolk for every 8 large potatoes. As well, using a blend of milk and cream makes them the creamiest potatoes in the world. But only for special occasions!

BERTON AND CLEMENT'S BAKED BEANS

SERVES 12 TO 16

Traditionally, I serve these beans over the Christmas holiday season, when I do my "Canadiana" dinner party. My family and friends keep asking me, "Do we have to wait until next December for those home-baked beans?" So now I include them with summertime barbecued spareribs, steaks and chicken.

This recipe, which I've developed over the years, is a combination of a recipe by Pierre Berton I had tried many years ago combined with my family baked bean recipe from the Maritimes. What a duo! Can't get more Canadiana than that! I usually put the beans in the oven on low overnight, and when we wake up in the morning, there is nothing like the aroma of the beans bubbling away. They are well worth the effort.

INGREDIENTS
6 cups small white beans
2 celery stalks, cut in half
½ cup chopped parsley
1 small onion, peeled and studded with 6 cloves
1 clove garlic, crushed
Pinch each of oregano, thyme, chili powder and salt
¾ lb salt pork or side bacon

STOCK
4 to 5 cups reserved bean stock
½ cup Heinz chili sauce
½ cup ketchup
1 can (5½ oz) tomato paste
1 cup molasses (not blackstrap)
¾ cup brown sugar
½ tsp dry mustard
Salt and pepper to taste
Dash Worcestershire sauce

TOPPING
½ cup dry sherry
Brown sugar

METHOD

Put the beans in a large Dutch oven and cover with water to a depth of at least 5 inches. Add the celery, parsley, onion, garlic and seasonings. Bring to boil and simmer for about 1½ to 2 hours until the beans are tender. Don't overcook. Remove pot from heat and ladle the beans into a bowl. Chop the celery and onion and add to bowl. Discard cloves, but save all the bean stock.

Cut the salt pork in small cubes and rinse in water to remove excess salt. Layer the pork or bacon with the beans in a bean crock and store in the refrigerator.

Combine 4 to 5 cups of the reserved stock with the rest of the stock ingredients and store in the refrigerator. When ready to bake, pour stock over beans in the crock just to cover. If needed, use more reserved stock or add water. Seal the lid well with foil, and bake at 250°F for about 8 hours, or until thick but still moist. About half an hour before done, remove cover and stir in sherry and sprinkle brown sugar on top.

PREPARATION TIME: 2 hours

DIANE'S SECRETS

If the beans become too thick in the refrigerator before serving, just add a little water. Any leftover beans can be frozen. Heinz chili sauce is the only chili sauce to use for these beans.

THE ULTIMATE MACARONI AND CHEESE

One of the "Hall of Fame" comfort foods is macaroni and cheese. And what makes a perfect macaroni and cheese casserole? The basic ingredients are usually a good-quality macaroni noodle, a medium white sauce, plenty of Cheddar cheese, a shot each of Tabasco and Worcestershire sauce and bread crumbs on top. The big difference between a "not bad" and a "mucho grando" macaroni and cheese is how creamy and cheesy it is. To our old family recipe, I've updated this classic by adding Parmesan and chèvre cheeses, but if you prefer the good old tried-and-true, stick with just the Cheddar!

INGREDIENTS
1 tbsp salt
1 lb (about 4 cups) macaroni or small
    penne style noodles
½ cup butter
½ cup flour
½ cup onions, finely chopped
1 tsp salt
2 tsp Dijon mustard
½ tsp Worcestershire sauce
Dash Tabasco
Dash pepper
4 cups milk
3 cups grated old Cheddar cheese
1 cup fresh grated Parmesan cheese
1 cup chèvre cheese, crumbled

TOPPING
1½ cups dry bread crumbs
½ cup Parmesan cheese
1 tsp Hungarian or sweet paprika
⅓ cup melted butter

METHOD

In a large 4-quart stockpot, bring about 3 quarts water and the 1 tbsp salt to a rolling boil. Add the macaroni slowly and bring to a boil. Cook according to the package directions. Drain well.

While the macaroni is cooking, melt the butter in a saucepan over medium heat. Add the flour, onions, 1 tsp salt, mustard, Worcestershire sauce, Tabasco and pepper. Stir to blend well for a few minutes, then add the milk slowly, stirring constantly until smooth and thickened. Add the cheeses and stir until melted. Add the sauce to the macaroni and pour into a greased 2½-quart casserole.

Combine the crumbs, Parmesan cheese and paprika and blend in the butter. Spread evenly on top of the macaroni mixture.

Bake at 375°F for 35 to 45 minutes or until golden and hot.

PREPARATION TIME: 35 minutes

Less fat: Decrease the amount of cheese, and choose low-fat varieties. Eliminate butter from the topping. Or try Vicki's French Macaroni Gratin on page 203!

 DIANE'S SECRETS

This dish can be refrigerated before baking.
To serve, bring to room temperature and cook according to directions. When reheating this dish, the macaroni and cheese will start to thicken and absorb the sauce. Puncture a few holes in the casserole and pour in a little more milk to prevent it from drying out.

MUSHROOM AND CHEESE STRATA

Strata, bread pudding, bread soufflé or sandwich bake: whatever you call it, it dates back to the early settlers of Canada. Back then, every scratch of leftover food was used in a casserole-style dish, and the base ingredients always included bread, milk and eggs. This total comfort food, popular in the fifties and sixties, has come full circle with a major comeback in the nineties. It's great for entertaining because it can be made hours ahead, or even the night before serving.

I've added a French twist by adding Emmentaler or Gruyère cheese, but sharp Cheddar, Monterey or fontina is also tasty. You can also enhance it with a cup of cubed baked ham.

INGREDIENTS
10 cups French bread, crusts removed, cut
    into ¾-inch cubes
1 cup grated Parmesan cheese
1½ cups grated Emmentaler or Gruyère cheese,
    or combination of both
3 tbsp olive oil
4 cups mushrooms, sliced
1 large leek, white part only, cleaned,
    sliced in julienne strips, then coarsely
    chopped (about ½ cup)
½ cup shallots or white onions, coarsely chopped
1 tbsp olive oil
6 large eggs
3 cups milk
1 tsp Dijon mustard
Salt and pepper to taste
¼ tsp sweet paprika
¾ cup grated Parmesan cheese

METHOD

Prepare the French bread. Mix together the 1 cup Parmesan cheese, and Emmentaler or Gruyère cheeses. Set aside.

Heat the 3 tbsp olive oil in a sauté pan, add mushrooms and sauté until softened. Remove from pan. Sauté the leeks and shallots in the 1 tbsp of olive oil until softened. Add to the mushroom mixture and set aside.

In a mixing bowl, combine eggs, milk, mustard, salt, pepper and paprika and whisk well to blend.

Layer ⅓ each of the bread, cheese mixture and the mushroom mixture in a buttered 13x9x2-inch pan or 2-quart casserole. Repeat 2 times. Pour the egg and milk mixture evenly over the casserole, and lightly press down. Cover pan and refrigerate for 6 to 8 hours or overnight. Remove from refrigerator about an hour ahead of baking. Sprinkle the remaining ¾ cup Parmesan cheese evenly over the top.

Bake in a 350°F oven for 50 to 60 minutes, or until a knife inserted into it comes out clean. It should be golden on top and puffed.

Less fat: Reduce the cheese and use skim milk.

PREPARATION TIME: 40 minutes

DIANE'S SECRETS

This dish makes a great brunch along with bagels, croissants, cream cheese, jams, platter of fresh fruit, juices and plenty of coffee. It also works as an impromptu dinner with a green salad, country bread and a good bottle of wine! Stuffed Tomatoes à la Provençale (page 197) is a wonderful complement. Try a combination of mushrooms such as portabello, shittake, chanterelle and/or oyster.

MAMA TOMATO'S OLD-FASHIONED MEAT LOAF

SERVES 10 TO 12

No one ever tires of meat loaf. When we opened the Tomato Café, we just had to include Mom's meat loaf on our special blue plate of the day. We served it with Garlic Mashed Potatoes (page 26) and canned creamed corn! Our customers would always phone to find out what day we were featuring it, then they would return the day after for our meat loaf sandwiches. Mom would always add rolled oats (instead of the more usual bread crumbs), cream of tomato soup and chili sauce to her meat loaf. The piquant sauce topping is a must as well.

INGREDIENTS
1 medium onion, coarsely chopped
2 tbsp butter
3 lb ground beef
¾ cup cream of tomato soup
¼ cup ketchup
¼ cup Heinz chili sauce
2 tbsp Dijon mustard
Salt and pepper to taste
2 tsp Worcestershire sauce
1 tsp HP sauce
Dash Tabasco
3 large eggs, slightly beaten
½ cup rolled oats (not the instant variety)
½ cup milk

PIQUANT SAUCE
2 cups ketchup
½ cup Heinz chili sauce
Generous shot each of Tabasco, Worcestershire
    sauce, and HP sauce
3 tbsp brown sugar

METHOD

MEAT LOAF

Sauté the onion in the butter until golden. In a bowl, mix together the ground beef, onion mixture, tomato soup, ketchup, chili sauce, mustard, salt and pepper, Worcestershire sauce, HP sauce and Tabasco. Set aside.

In another large bowl, mix together the eggs, rolled oats, and milk. Let stand a few minutes and add the beef mixture, blending well by hand until thoroughly mixed. Divide evenly between two 9x5-inch well-greased loaf pans, pressing down well. Top each loaf pan with about 1¼ cups of piquant sauce.

Bake in a 375°F oven for 1 to 1¼ hours, or until the beef is not pink. Drain off the excess juices and serve immediately.

PIQUANT SAUCE

Blend all ingredients well. (This sauce keeps refrigerated for several days. Makes about 3 cups, enough for topping and to serve on the side.)

PREPARATION TIME: 20 minutes

Less fat: Use extra-lean ground beef, and drain off the fat and juices from the pans after cooking.

DIANE'S SECRETS

This recipe makes about 6 slices per loaf, leaving enough for the next day's meat loaf sandwiches! Slice the loaf ¼-inch thick. Spread some mayonnaise on 2 slices of sourdough or French bread. On one half add lettuce. Top with 2 slices of meat loaf, a little piquant sauce, 3 slices tomatoes, and salt and pepper. Cover with the second slice of bread, and enjoy!

CHICKEN À LA KING

If there was ever a luncheon or dinner party dish defining the fifties, it was definitely this one. Served in patty shells on your best china, with fresh asparagus or a jellied salad on the side, it was "Oh so chic!" And when we did the photo shoots for this book and tasted this old classic, it was "Oh so good!"

In the fifties, there were no red peppers, only green. Canned red pimentos and green peppers were used, but I substitute finely chopped red peppers in place of both. This dish is usually served on puff pastry patty shells or baking powder biscuits. You can find patty shells in a French or specialty bakery.

INGREDIENTS
¼ cup butter
2 cups mushrooms, sliced
½ cup sweet red pepper, finely chopped
¼ cup flour
2 cups milk
½ cup chicken stock
Salt and pepper to taste
Pinch sweet paprika
1 large egg yolk, slightly beaten
2 tbsp dry sherry
2 tsp lemon juice
2 cups cooked chicken breasts
  (about 2 double breasts)
4 patty shells

METHOD

To bake the chicken breasts, place two double breasts (deboned and skinned) in a small casserole and cover with foil. Roast at 350°F for 15 minutes, then remove cover. Continue roasting for 15 minutes or until no pink juices appear. Cool and cut into cubes.

Meanwhile, in a large fry pan, melt the butter and sauté the mushrooms and red pepper a few minutes until softened. Add the flour, blending well. Gradually add the milk and chicken stock. Simmer on low, stirring constantly, until thickened. Add the salt, pepper and paprika. Remove a few spoonfuls of the mixture and blend with the slightly beaten egg yolk, then blend into the hot mixture. Add the sherry and lemon juice and stir for a few minutes. Add the cooked chicken. Cool.

Before serving, heat the mixture in a casserole in a 350°F oven for about 30 minutes or until bubbly. The sauce will be thick; if necessary, thin with a little milk.

Heat the patty shells about 5 minutes in a 350°F oven, just to heat through, before serving. Place a patty shell on each plate, fill to the top with the chicken mixture and serve immediately.

Less fat: Use skim milk and eliminate the egg yolk (the sauce will be thinner).

PREPARATION TIME: 35 minutes

DIANE'S SECRETS

If you can't find patty shells and haven't time to make baking powder biscuits, toast a 1-inch thick slice of sourdough or French bread per serving. Top with the chicken. This recipe can be prepared several hours ahead of serving – even the night before. Just reheat as directed before serving.

JENNIFER AND RAND'S TUNA NOODLE CASSEROLE

SERVES 4

After our honeymoon, during which Doug and I survived on a diet of canned tuna, instant rice and cream of mushroom soup, it took me a few years to even look at another tuna casserole. However, as our children grew up, I relied on this quick dish that they always gobbled up! And whenever I mentioned to people that I was revisiting the fifties and sixties food scene for this book, they all exclaimed, "You've got to put in a tuna casserole!" This version of an old classic is a combination of a recipe from the *Sunset Magazine* casserole series and Mom's old Imperial Order Daughters of the Empire cookbook, published by the Louisbourg, Nova Scotia chapter, circa 1942! So with happy memories of the "old faithful" tuna casserole, this is for our children, Jennifer and Rand, with love.

INGREDIENTS
1 cup sliced mushrooms,
1 tbsp olive oil
3 cups cooked noodles
1 to 2 cans (6- or 7-oz size) solid white tuna, drained, broken into chunks
2 hard boiled eggs, coarsely chopped (optional)
1 can (10½ oz) cream of mushroom soup
¾ cup milk
1 tsp dried dill, or 2 tbsp fresh, chopped
2 tbsp dry sherry (optional)
Salt and pepper to taste

TOPPING
¾ cup fresh bread crumbs
3 tbsp melted butter
¼ cup grated Parmesan cheese
Pinch paprika

METHOD

To make topping, blend together all ingredients. Set aside.

In a small fry pan, sauté mushrooms in olive oil. In a buttered casserole, layer noodles, tuna, sautéed mushrooms and eggs, ending with the noodles on top. In a bowl, blend the soup, milk, dill, sherry, salt and pepper. Pour over the layers, and sprinkle topping mixture evenly over all. Refrigerate until ready to bake.

Bake uncovered at 350°F for 30 to 35 minutes or until golden and hot.

PREPARATION TIME: 20 minutes

Less fat: Use skim milk and eliminate butter from the topping.

DIANE'S SECRETS *If desired, add about ½ cup sautéed chopped onions. If the casserole seems dry, add a little more milk when baking.*

STEAK SUPERB, CALIFORNIA-STYLE

When I was an international athlete, the thing to eat before any major competition was a thick steak, supposedly to provide energy. Years later nutritionists announced that pasta, not high-protein foods, provided the needed energy before competition.

This recipe brought rave reviews from everyone when we served it to the interns from Doug's hospital and their wives during our stay in San Francisco in 1959, and still today, when I feel the urge for a juicy, barbecued steak, this is what I serve. Try it with Potatoes Romanoff (page 24), corn on the cob, and Doug's Favourite Salad Deluxe (page 20).

INGREDIENTS
3 to 3½ lb sirloin steak, cut 1½ to 2 inches thick
½ cup butter
¼ cup chopped parsley
¼ cup finely chopped onion
2 tsp Worcestershire sauce
¼ tsp Dijon mustard
Pinch salt
½ tsp pepper

METHOD

In a saucepan, combine all ingredients except the steak and heat until the butter melts. Refrigerate overnight, if desired. Reheat before using.

To grill the steak, slash the fat edges every inch or so. Prepare the barbecue and grease the barbecue rack with a little oil. Place the steak on the rack, about 4 inches from source of heat. Grill about 10 minutes each side for rare meat; 12 to 14 minutes each side for medium, brushing with the sauce several times during grilling. To check if done, make a small slit in the centre of the steak and note the colour. Red equals rare; pink is medium; and grey means well done. Serve sliced on the diagonal about ⅓ inch thick. Serve immediately.

Less fat: Reduce the amount of butter used.

PREPARATION TIME: 10 minutes

DIANE'S SECRETS

Sirloin steaks are best. Be sure to pre-order the steaks from your butcher to ensure the proper thickness.

One of the most emotional and memorable times of my life was during the Opening Ceremonies of the 1956 Olympic Games in Melbourne, Australia, when I represented Canada as a member of our track and field team. As our Canadian team started down the ramp to enter the massive Olympic Stadium, we could hear the roar of 70,000 fans welcoming the athletes representing 150 nations. As I entered the stadium for the first time, I spotted our Canadian flag waving in the wind. At that moment, it hit me for the first time: "I'm in the Olympic Games!" First I waved with excitement, then I started to cry, then I laughed with joy. I thought back to the early days of training in Moncton with my twin brother David, with my coaches, Meddy Cormier, Bill Kelliher, Mom, Dad, and brother Joel, who were so supportive. I thought of our moving to Montreal where I was coached by a former Olympian, Jack Carrol, and of the Olympic Trials when I was officially named to the team. As the band played "O Canada" our team turned and saluted to the Royal Box. We then took our places to wait for the Olympic torchbearer to light the Olympic flame to signify "Let the Games begin!" It was a very proud moment in my life. Having been a member of our Canadian Olympic Team as an official at four more Olympic Games, those very same warm, proud feelings return as we parade around the Olympic Stadium. ✍

Lobster Tales

My brother Joel is well known throughout Nova Scotia and the Maritimes as a former member of Parliament, now retired. He is also famous for his Halifax lobster feeds. Joel and his wife Ruth have entertained diplomats and friends from around the world, and they are still singing the praises of Joey's amazing lobsters. Everyone who has tasted them wants to know his secret! So for all you lobster aficionados, here is everything you ever wanted to know and more, straight from Joel, about preparing and presenting the most succulent lobsters you will ever have the joy of eating!

PREPARING LOBSTERS – JOEL-STYLE

The best results are attained using premium hardshelled lobsters. The hardshell lobster has a much greater meat content and cooks more evenly. A good weight is 1¼ to 1½ lb, as this size lobster fits best in most pots. My pot is a medium weight and can easily accommodate six of this size lobster.

To speed up the process, I pre-boil the water in the electric kettle and add to the pot as it heats up at maximum heat level. To prevent boiling over, do not fill above the three-quarter level.

Once the water boils, add 1 tbsp of salt for every quart of water and 1 tsp of brown sugar for each lobster in the pot. A lobster fisherman from the South Shore area of Nova Scotia told me the brown sugar adds a special touch, firming the meat and enhancing the flavour. But don't be tempted to add more than 1 tsp per lobster; in this case, more is not better!

Put the lobsters into the boiling water head first. At this point, the boil will come off the water. There are two schools of thought about when you should start your timing: when the lobsters go in or when the pot returns to boil. My experience with today's modern stoves is that at high heat, the water quickly returns to boiling. I set my timer when I see the first signs of the water nearing the boiling point. Usually, small bubbles start to appear. For 1 lb lobsters, cook 14 to 15 minutes; for 1¼ to 1½ lb lobsters, 17 to 18 minutes; and for 1½ to 2 lb lobsters, 20 to 22 minutes. Twice during the process, using tongs, I move the lobsters from the bottom to the top.

When the time is up, immediately remove the lobsters from the pot. For easier handling, rinse them briefly under cold tap water, then place them on a tray. Using a nutcracker, break open the claws and knuckles, making sure not to separate them from the lobster. Turn over, and using a large, sharp knife, split open the tail section and drain off the water collected inside. This process makes the eating, for you and your guests, much easier and far less messy.

Depending on how many lobsters you are serving, you will be cooking them in batches. Before starting on a new batch, bring the water back to the three-quarter level and add half the amount of salt and brown sugar as in the first batch. Follow the same steps as above. If you have a few batches, you don't need to rinse them as they will have time to cool on their own.

While the lobsters are boiling, I melt lots of butter, slice Ruth's brown bread warm out of the oven (see Anne Murray's Brown Bread, page 56), toss the salad and open the wine and beer. We provide a large lobster bib for each guest, many paper napkins, and add a few miniature lobster pots for the melted butter, nutcrackers, picks, lobster scissors, and empty bowls for the shells.

Most of the lobster can be eaten including the body where you will find some of the most tender meat. You have to work for it though! Do not eat the head, and be sure to remove the small vein from the tail.

As some people find the process of putting live lobsters in boiling water rather difficult, I can pass on to you a recommendation from my fishermen friends. I hypnotize the lobsters and they go into a deep sleep! The process works and your lobsters go into the pot relaxed and unaware of their fate. First, place the live lobster on its head on the floor, with its claws spread out behind it and its tail in the air. Hold the lobster and begin to slowly stroke its back. It will gradually relax and remain immobile on its head. Once it is relaxed and "sleeping," put it down and leave it alone; it will not move. My record is 10 totally relaxed lobsters lined up in a row! To speed things up I have found that humming the same tune I used to rock my children to sleep works very well. I have not determined whether it is the stroking or my singing that has the strongest influence over the lobster, but I know it works! It takes a little patience and practice, but you will impress your guests with your obvious sensitivity for the plight of the lobster! ✑

RUTH'S NOVA SCOTIA SEAFOOD CASSEROLE

SERVES 6 TO 8

Ruth Matheson, my sister-in-law, knows that whenever Doug and I visit Halifax, we cannot leave without having her seafood casserole. As well, her sister Nancy Locke and her husband Bud have treated us to this dish that has been in their family for decades. Ruth says that this casserole has survived from the days when rich food was not considered something to be avoided. The fresh flavours of the seafood tantalize you with every bite. As an added bonus, it is quick and easy to make! Ruth suggests cooking this casserole in a dish you can take straight to the table.

A salad of wild greens with a light vinaigrette dressing makes an ideal starter. I wouldn't bother with appetizers, as this dish is always the star of the dinner.

INGREDIENTS
6 slices white bread, crusts removed, each piece
    cut in 4 squares
4 lb fresh fish, a combination of haddock or any
    white fish, scallops, and lobster or shrimp

SAUCE
1 cup butter
1 cup flour
1½ tsp salt
Pinch pepper
4 cups milk

CROUTON TOPPING
6 slices white bread with crusts, cut in 1-inch pieces
½ tsp Hungarian or sweet paprika
3 tbsp melted butter

METHOD

SAUCE

In a saucepan, melt the butter and add the flour, salt and pepper, stirring constantly a few minutes to blend well. Add the milk gradually, stirring constantly until blended. Continue to stir over medium heat, until thickened and smooth. Set aside.

This sauce can be prepared a day ahead and refrigerated. Remove from refrigerator an hour before cooking.

CROUTON TOPPING

Put the bread pieces in a bowl and toss with the paprika, then the melted butter to coat the pieces. Set aside.

TO ASSEMBLE

Lightly butter a 2-quart casserole. Place the 24 squares of the bread (without crusts) around the outside of the casserole, not on the bottom.

In a bowl, toss the three fish together. Place a layer of the fish on the bottom of the casserole. Pour some of the sauce over top. Continue layering fish and sauce, ending with the sauce. Top the casserole with the paprika croutons. At this point, you can refrigerate the dish for a few hours until ready to reheat.

Bake at 375°F for 40 to 45 minutes or until hot and croutons are golden. If the croutons brown too soon, cover the casserole with foil.

PREPARATION TIME: 40 minutes

Less fat: Every Nova Scotian who makes this specialty dish would cover me with cod liver oil if I changed this recipe one little bit! Although it does include quite a bit of butter, it can't hurt to serve this dish every once in a while on a special occasion, like at a dinner party that features a menu of Nova Scotia delights. Don't forget to include the bagpipes! It is rich, so serve small portions to start with.

DIANE'S SECRETS
Fresh blanched asparagus sprinkled with lemon juice and pepper is a perfect complement to this regal dish!

SPANISH PAELLA

SERVES 8 TO 10

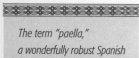

The term "paella,"
a wonderfully robust Spanish
dish, comes from the pan in
which it is made. These
pans are usually about 14
to 15 inches in diameter,
with two handles. You can
purchase the pans in most
specialty cooking shops.
Paella can also be made in
any large skillet or Dutch
oven cookware made of
heavy aluminum. ℬ

Paella was the diva of many summertime parties during our stay in San Francisco in 1959. After all these years, paella is once again a popular choice for casual entertaining.

The basis of the paella is rice with a hint of the distinct saffron spice. It can include chicken, chorizo sausage, pork, fresh seafood, onions, garlic, pimentos and mushrooms all sautéed in the best of Spanish olive oil. It can be cooked entirely on top of the heat or in the oven, which is easier to control. (If you have a gas burner large enough to hold the paella pan, it will give you that wonderful caramelized bottom characteristic of the authentic paella.) A although this dish appears to be a lot of work, it can be prepared ahead of time, making your dinner party more fun for you.

INGREDIENTS
¼ cup light olive oil
2 chicken breasts, boned and skinned,
    cut into 1-inch pieces
½ lb chorizo or pepperoni sausage, cut into pieces
1 lb boneless pork, cut into 1-inch pieces
1 large onion, finely chopped
1 red pepper, coarsely chopped
¼ lb fresh mushrooms, sliced
3 cloves garlic, crushed
¼ tsp saffron powder or 1 tsp saffron threads,
    soaked in ¼ cup chicken stock
¼ tsp oregano
3 cups long-grain white rice
8 cups chicken stock
¼ cup brandy
½ lb fresh red snapper or other white fish,
    cut into 2-inch pieces
½ lb scallops, sliced in half (optional)
Salt and pepper to taste
1 lb raw medium-size prawns, peeled
1½ cups fresh or frozen peas
2 medium tomatoes, peeled and seeded
24 baby clams
2 canned or bottled pimentos, thinly sliced

2 lemons, sliced into wedges
½ cup stuffed green Spanish olives

METHOD

Heat the olive oil in a large shallow pan and sauté the chicken, sausage and pork until golden. Remove and set aside. Sauté the onion, red pepper and mushrooms for a few minutes, then add the garlic, saffron, oregano, and rice and sauté for about 5 minutes more. Return the meats to the pan with the rice and vegetable mixture. The paella can be prepared ahead to this point and refrigerated.

Half an hour before guests arrive, heat the oven to 400°F. Add the stock, brandy, fish and scallops to the meat and rice mixture in your large pan. Salt and pepper to taste. Bring to a boil, cover with foil and put into the oven. Bake for about 20 minutes. Remove the foil and bake for about 10 more minutes.

Add the prawns, stirring slightly. Add the peas and tomatoes. Bake another 5 to 10 minutes or until the prawns are cooked and the stock has just about absorbed all the rice and is cooked. Do not overcook; the paella should be moist, not dry. Add more chicken stock if necessary.

Meanwhile, steam the clams separately, discarding any that don't open. Add clams to the paella the last 5 minutes and bake uncovered. When finished, cover with foil to keep moist until ready to serve.

To serve, decorate the top with the pimentos, lemons and ripe olives.

PREPARATION TIME: 1 hour

DIANE'S SECRETS

This is a great dish for entertaining because of the one main dish. Pick up a hearty country bread and one of Spain's most popular cheeses, the aged Manchego, which you can find in specialty cheese markets. Add some Spanish Manzanilla olives and roasted almonds and you have the perfect appetizers to complement a well-chilled Spanish sherry or fruity Sangria (see my delightful recipe for Spanish Sangria, page 13). My dessert choice is Starllie's Almond Cake (page 220) with fresh fruit and sorbets.

CORINNE'S NOVA SCOTIA COD CAKES

SERVES 6

I think most Maritimers have eaten tons of cod cakes during their lifetime. We always knew at home when we were having cod cakes because the whole house would smell of salty fish! For that reason, I don't recommend preparing them if you are having a party the next evening, or if you are selling your house, but boy are they good! My sister-in-law, Dianne Matheson in Toronto, passed on to me Corinne and Bruce Murray's favourite cod cake recipe from their native Nova Scotia. It's truly a Maritime treasure, and well worth the ritual of preparing the codfish.

INGREDIENTS
1 lb boneless salt cod
8 to 10 medium-size potatoes
1 egg
2 tbsp butter (approx.)
1 onion, well ground
Summer savory or ground savory (or both)
Cornmeal or flour

METHOD

The night before serving, soak the salt cod in water. In the morning, drain well, reserving the liquid. Pour fresh water over the cod and boil until soft, about 1 hour.

Peel the potatoes, and boil them in reserved cod water 25 to 30 minutes until soft. Drain and mash. Break the egg into the potatoes and add the butter, onion, savory and cooked salt cod. Mix well. (The mixture will be sticky.)

Wet your hands for easier handling of the batter and form the mixture into 10 to 12 medium-size patties. Dip each patty in cornmeal or flour (or combination of both) to coat well. Fry patties in a little butter until golden brown on both sides and hot. Serve immediately with ketchup.

PREPARATION TIME: 25 minutes

DIANE'S SECRETS

Cod cakes can be refrigerated until ready to cook. Just layer them between sheets of waxed paper.

THE FONDUE PARTY

Fondue parties were wildly popular in the fifties and sixties. Everyone had a fondue set, which included the fondue pot and dinner plates with a large section for the meat, smaller sections for the sauces, and multi-coloured forks for each person to know whose meat was cooking. Secondhand stores today are selling out of these sets, and kitchen shops are starting to stock them as fondue parties enjoy a revival.

Fondue parties offer a leisurely paced style of entertaining. They're a lot of fun and easy to set up. I usually like to serve a salad before we start the fondue going, either a Caesar or wild greens with a light vinaigrette. Guests can continue to nibble on the salad as the meats are cooking. A tart lemon dessert is my choice for the finale.

I like to have 2 to 3 fondue pots going at once for over 4 people. Any deep chafing dish will work, but it is important to have the Sterno heating units lit under the chafing dishes to keep the oil hot. Place your sauces in attractive bowls along the table so your guests can help themselves.

Small ramekins are perfect for holding the sauces. If you don't have the special fondue plates, provide each guest with a small ramekin for each of the sauces you serve.

For a fun fondue appetizer, see my recipe for Après-Ski Cheese Fondue (page 14).

YOU'LL NEED
Fondue pots
Tins of Sterno for heat (have extra on hand)
Vegetable oil (not olive oil)
Beef tenderloin and/or chicken breasts
Jumbo shrimp, peeled and deveined
Small button mushrooms, stems removed
Assorted sauces

For each person, allow about ½ lb of beef tenderloin, 1 chicken breast, 5 to 6 jumbo shrimp and 3 to 4 mushrooms per person. Have a separate pot for cooking the fish.

METHOD
Trim off the excess fat and cut the beef into bite-size pieces. Cut the chicken breasts into 1-inch cubes. Fill the fondue pot no more than

two-thirds full with the oil. Heat the oil until a piece of meat starts to simmer when dropped in.

TO COOK

Each guest spears a steak cube, chicken or prawn with a fondue fork, and sets it in the oil until cooked to their likeness, usually about 30 seconds. Mushrooms cook in just a few seconds.

PREPARATION TIME: 1 hour for meat, sauces and vegetables.

ASSORTED FONDUE SAUCES

SATAY SAUCE

MAKES ABOUT 2 CUPS

INGREDIENTS
1 cup creamy or crunchy peanut butter
1 cup canned coconut milk
1/3 cup chicken stock
3 tbsp soy sauce
2 cloves garlic, minced
Zest and juice of 1 lemon
3 tbsp Chinese sweet chili sauce
1 tbsp brown sugar
2 tbsp pure dark sesame oil

METHOD

Combine all the ingredients in a food processor, reserving a quarter of the coconut milk and stock. Blend until creamy. If the sauce is too thick (it should be medium-thick), dilute with some of the reserved liquids. Serve warm or at room temperature. Can be made 3 to 4 days ahead and refrigerated. If it becomes too thick from the refrigeration, add a little hot water or chicken stock to thin it out.

SPICY STEAK SAUCE

MAKES ABOUT 1 CUP

INGREDIENTS
1 cup mayonnaise
1 tbsp HP sauce
1 tbsp Worcestershire sauce
6 tbsp chili sauce
Several dashes Tabasco

METHOD
Blend all ingredients well.
Can be made 2 to 3 days ahead and refrigerated.

HOT MARMALADE DIP

MAKES ABOUT 1 CUP

INGREDIENTS
½ cup orange marmalade
¼ cup lemon juice
¼ cup soy sauce
1 clove garlic, finely crushed
⅛ tsp ground ginger
½ tsp cornstarch
1 tbsp water

METHOD
In a saucepan, combine the first five ingredients and bring to a boil. Dissolve the cornstarch in the water, then add to the hot sauce and cook until thickened, stirring constantly. Can be made 1 to 2 days ahead and refrigerated. Reheat just before serving.

MOCK BÉARNAISE SAUCE

This is a simple version of the original Béarnaise sauce

INGREDIENTS
2 cups mayonnaise
¼ cup fresh tarragon, finely chopped
3 tbsp white wine vinegar
1 tsp Dijon mustard
⅓ cup chopped shallots or green onions

METHOD
In a food processor or blender, combine all ingredients and blend for a few seconds. Can be made 1 to 2 days ahead and refrigerated.

Less fat: Chicken, vegetable or fish stock can be substituted for the oil. Choose the lower-fat sauces (Hot Marmalade Dip and Yogurt Dip). Chutneys also make a great dip, and try Piquant Sauce (page 31).

YOGURT DIP

INGREDIENTS
1 cup unflavoured yogurt
⅓ cup chopped dill
1 tbsp grainy Dijon mustard

METHOD
Stir together all ingredients.

DIANE'S SECRETS — *Whenever I do a fondue evening, I don't bother with appetizers. We move right to the table, ignite the sterno and let the party begin!*

GRANDMOTHER'S TEA BISCUITS OR SCONES

These biscuits have been called tea biscuits, scones or baking powder biscuits. Whatever you call them, they are as popular today as they were in the 1800s. My grandmothers, Gramma Shoove and Gramma MacDonald, must have made hundreds of tea biscuits during their lifetime, as they lived well into their eighties and nineties. When their mothers made biscuits in the late 1800s, they had to make their own baking powder by combining ground rice, soda and tartaric acid.

Served with homemade jams, Devonshire cream, cream cheese or mascarpone cheese, baking powder biscuits are still as popular as ever. At our Tomato Fresh Food Café they have been on the menu from the first day we opened. At around 8 a.m. every day, I would mix up the batter and pop them in oven to be warm and ready when we opened the doors for our customers.

INGREDIENTS
2½ cups all-purpose flour
1 tbsp baking powder
½ tsp baking soda
2 tbsp granulated sugar
½ tsp salt
½ cup chilled butter, cut into bits
1 cup dried fruit (raisins, apricots, cranberries, cherries)
1 large egg
1 cup buttermilk

EGG WASH
Beat together lightly:
1 large egg
1 tbsp milk, slightly beaten

METHOD

In a bowl, combine the flour, baking powder, baking soda, sugar and salt. Cut in the butter until well blended. Add the fruit. In a separate bowl, combine the egg and the buttermilk and beat well. Add all at once to the flour mixture, stirring lightly just to form a ball. Don't overmix!

Turn the dough out onto a floured surface and knead gently to form a smooth, soft dough. Roll out into a circle about ¾-inch thick. Cut into small rounds about 2½ inches across and place on a cookie sheet. Brush tops with egg wash and bake at 400° F for 12 to 15 minutes, or until baked through and golden.

STRAWBERRY SHORTCAKE

Add 1 tsp vanilla to milk. Omit fruit.

SAVOURY BISCUITS

Add 1 cup Cheddar, Parmesan, or fontina cheese to the dry batter. Omit fruit.

PREPARATION TIME: 10 minutes

Why is it that we all still crave the breads, biscuits, desserts and cakes that our mothers and grandmothers baked? I think it's because they weren't mass produced, they were made just for us. It was always such a proud moment when they were presented to us. We would sit, wondering, "What did she bake for us today"? These wonderful recipes for biscuits and bread will fill your home with the warm memories of Mom's, or Grandma's, kitchen. ✄

DIANE'S SECRETS

Always serve the biscuits warmed in the oven. Just wrap them in foil and reheat at 350°F for about 10 minutes or until warmed. Never heat these biscuits in the microwave.

ANNE'S BROWN BREAD

MAKES 2 LOAVES

This recipe originated from Anne Murray's mother's kitchen, and it's Anne's favourite bread. It has also become our "Matheson" Clan's ultimate bread to have with Joel's lobsters (see Preparing Lobsters, page 42). Ruth always doubles this recipe, because otherwise the bread just disappears! It freezes well, so you can always have a loaf on hand.

Forget French baguettes, this sensational bread from Nova Scotia wins hands down! Don't be intimidated by making breads using yeast; this recipe is foolproof.

INGREDIENTS
1 shredded wheat biscuit, crumbled
½ cup grape nut cereal
2 tbsp butter
⅓ cup brown sugar
⅓ cup molasses (not blackstrap)
1½ tsp salt
1 cup milk
1 cup water
1 tsp sugar
½ cup warm water
1 tbsp dry yeast
6 cups (approx.) all-purpose flour
¾ cup wheat germ (optional)

DIANE'S SECRETS

Try this bread toasted with homemade jam. Marvellous!

METHOD
In a large bowl, mix together the first 8 ingredients. Mix the sugar with warm water and dissolve the yeast in it. Add the yeast mixture to the bowl and stir well. Add the flour, using just enough to form a stiff dough, kneading lightly. Knead in wheat germ.

Put dough in a greased bowl, cover with a damp cloth and leave to rise until double in bulk, about 1½ hours. Punch down and divide dough into two. Shape into loaves and place in greased 9x5-inch loaf pans. Leave to rise until double, about 30 to 40 minutes.

Bake at 375°F for 50 minutes, or until the loaves sound hollow when tapped on the bottom. Brush loaves with butter.

PREPARATION TIME: 25 minutes, plus rising time

Zest for Life   ஃ   *Plate # 1*

Zest for Life   ♾   *Plate # 3*

Plate # 4   *Zest for Life*

Zest for Life ❧ *Plate # 5*

MONIQUE AND DIANE'S LEMON CURD TART • 58

Plate # 6   *Zest for Life*

Zest for Life ❧ *Plate # 7*

QUICHE LORRAINE TARTLETS • 72

Plate # 8   *Zest for Life*

Zest for Life   *Plate # 9*

Plate # 10 ❧ *Zest for Life*

Plate # 14   *Zest for Life*

Zest for Life   &   *Plate # 15*

CHOCOLATE BROWNIE PUDDING

SERVES 6

Henry Winkler, better known as the Fonz, raved about our brownies at the Tomato. I'd like to think he'd enjoy this as much or more! It's actually a chocolate cake with its own chocolate pudding. Serve warm with a scoop of vanilla ice cream.

INGREDIENTS
1 cup all-purpose flour
2 tsp baking powder
½ tsp salt
¾ cup granulated sugar
3 tbsp Dutch cocoa
½ cup milk
1 tsp vanilla
2 tbsp butter, melted

TOPPING
¼ cup Dutch cocoa
1½ cups brown sugar
1¾ cups hot water

METHOD

In a bowl, blend together the flour, baking powder, salt, sugar and cocoa. Make a well in the centre of the mixture and add milk, vanilla and butter. Mix gently until smooth. Don't overmix. Pour batter into greased 8x8-inch pan.

TOPPING

In a small bowl, whisk rapidly the cocoa, sugar and water for about 3 minutes. Pour over the batter in pan.

Heat oven to 350°F and bake for 35 to 40 minutes, or until the cake tests done and springs back when lightly touched. As the cake bakes, the batter will rise through the rich chocolate sauce. Serve warm.

PREPARATION TIME: 15 minutes

DIANE'S SECRETS *Make two, one won't be enough once you take your first bite! Can be made a day ahead, if desired. Reheat uncovered at 350°F for about 10 minutes or until warmed.*

Henry Winkler was in Vancouver in 1993 to direct a film. He tasted our brownies at his wrap party. The next day I received a phone call from his wife in Taluka Lake, California, requesting that we courier three dozen brownies that day to his home to surprise him. I thought someone was teasing me. But when she gave me her Visa number and told me that Henry had phoned her that morning to tell her he had just tasted the best brownies he had ever eaten, I yelled to my staff, "It's for real!" Then the fun began. In a mad rush we whipped them up, packaged them while warm, and then Jamie and I dashed off to the Federal Express office at the airport. They were delivered as promised, and since then they've been known as Fonzie's Brownies.

Less fat: Serve with low-fat frozen vanilla yogurt instead of ice cream.

MONIQUE AND DIANE'S LEMON CURD TART

SERVES 6 TO 8

Monique Barbeau is a family friend, raised in Vancouver, and the former Executive Chef of the prestigious Fuller's restaurant in Seattle. She is one of the top chefs in North America. Monique joined forces with me in 1995 for a major Vancouver fundraiser dinner for scholarships for women entering the food and hospitality profession, hosted by Les Dames d'Escoffier, Vancouver Chapter.

Whenever I have to bring sweets for a fundraiser, people always request Mom's lemon tarts. So, when Monique and I combined Mom's pastry recipe with her wonderfully tart lemon curd on this highly successful evening, the result was the best lemon curd tart in the world!

INGREDIENTS

CRUST
1 cup flour
¼ cup white sugar
⅓ cup butter
1 extra large egg, slightly beaten

FILLING
1¾ cups fresh lemon juice
Zest of 2 lemons, finely chopped
1½ cups white sugar
7 eggs
5 egg yolks
¾ cup cold, unsalted butter

METHOD

CRUST

Combine the flour and sugar and cut in the butter until the mixture resembles coarse meal. Stir in the egg, mixing well. Wrap and chill for about 30 minutes. Pat down and, using your hands, press the pastry evenly into bottom and up the sides of a 9-inch flan pan with removable sides. (It's easier to use your hands rather than trying to roll out the dough, as it is very soft.) Prick with a fork. Refrigerate for 30 minutes, then bake at 350°F for 8 to 10 minutes, or until slightly golden. Cool.

FILLING

In a double boiler or a mixing bowl placed over gently simmering water, whisk together the lemon juice, lemon zest, sugar, eggs and egg yolks. Whisk vigorously until the mixture has thickened to the consistency of a hollandaise sauce or until thick and creamy, about 5 to 7 minutes. Remove from the heat and whisk in the butter until it is melted. Pour the filling into the cooled crust to fill to the top, and let sit at room temperature for at least 1 hour or until set. Serve with fresh berries

> **PREPARATION TIME:** 45 minutes, including chilling the pie shell before baking

DIANE'S SECRETS

To get a head start, you can make the pie shell and filling a day ahead and store separately in the refrigerator overnight. The next day, fill the pie shell and refrigerate until ready to serve. You may have some filling left over; it's great with angel food cake or over vanilla ice cream or frozen yogurt!

BLUM'S COFFEE-TOFFEE PIE

Back in the late fifties, Sak's Fifth Avenue, just off Union Square in San Francisco, had the most fashionable ice cream parlour featuring their Blum's Coffee-Toffee Pie. I never did know where the name came from. All I know is that once in a while Doug and I would venture in and have a dish of their outstanding ice cream and a wedge of this pie! Returning to Vancouver, I served it to many friends at many dinner parties. It became the favourite dessert of a good friend, Susan Newson, who opened the first avant-garde catering company in Vancouver, Glorious Foods (and glorious they were!). It was a treat for me to pass on this dream of a dessert recipe to her.

INGREDIENTS

CRUST
½ package pie crust mix
¼ cup light brown sugar
¾ cup finely chopped pecans or walnuts
1 square unsweetened chocolate, grated
1 tbsp water
1 tsp vanilla

FILLING
½ cup soft butter
¾ cup white sugar
1 square unsweetened chocolate, melted and cooled
1 tbsp instant coffee
2 eggs

TOPPING
1 cup whipping cream
1 tbsp instant coffee
1 tbsp coffee liqueur (optional)
¼ cup icing sugar
Chocolate curls or crushed almond roca
    bars (about 4)

METHOD

CRUST

In medium-size bowl, combine the pie crust mix with the brown sugar, pecans or walnuts and grated chocolate. Add water and vanilla. With fork, mix until well blended. Turn into a well-greased 9-inch pie plate or springform pan, pressing pastry firmly against the bottom and sides.

Bake at 375°F for 10 to 15 minutes or until golden. Watch carefully! Cool on wire rack.

FILLING

With electric mixer at medium speed, beat the butter until creamy. Gradually add the sugar. Blend in the melted chocolate and the coffee. Add 1 egg; beat 5 minutes. Add second egg; beat 5 minutes more. Pour into baked pie shell. Cover. Refrigerate overnight.

TOPPING

In a large bowl, combine the whipping cream, coffee, coffee liqueur and icing sugar. Refrigerate for one hour, then beat until stiff, being careful not to turn it to butter. Decorate top of pie with this creamy mixture and garnish with chocolate curls or almond roca. Refrigerate for at least 2 hours before serving.

PREPARATION TIME: 30 minutes

 DIANE'S SECRETS   *You don't need to serve coffee with this pie!*

DIANE'S RUM BALLS

MAKES 9 TO 10 DOZEN

When I launched my first book, *Chef on the Run*, in the early eighties, I did a cross-Canada tour from Victoria, B.C., to Halifax, Nova Scotia. For all my television, radio and press interviews I presented the interviewers with a small box of my signature rum balls and the recipe. They were a big hit! I've made thousands of these tasty morsels since the early sixties. I still hear from people all across Canada and the United States who tell me they make the rum balls every holiday season, and they have become a tradition to give as gifts as well as to enjoy themselves. Their children pitch in to help make the rum balls, just as our children did over the years.

Make them weeks ahead and store them in the refrigerator. They need at least two weeks to mature – if you can wait that long! And make them small – they are powerful!

INGREDIENTS
12 oz semi-sweet chocolate, melted
1 cup sour cream
½ cup almond paste (Marzipan)
Pinch salt
8 cups finely crushed Christie's vanilla wafers
   (approx. 4 boxes)
3 cups icing sugar
1½ cups melted butter
⅔ cup Dutch cocoa
1½ cups white rum
2 cups pecans, finely chopped
Pure chocolate shot or sprinkles
   (approx. 5 to 6 cups)

62   *Desserts / Zest for Life*

METHOD

In a food processor, combine the melted chocolate, sour cream, almond paste and salt. Cream well and set aside. In a separate bowl, combine the wafers and the rest of the ingredients, except for the chocolate shot. Mix until it holds its shape. Add the chocolate-sour cream mixture and knead with your hands until blended and soft. Place in the refrigerator until firm enough to form small balls in the palm of your hand, yet soft enough to pick up the chocolate shot. The batter can be made the day ahead, if desired.

To form the rum balls: Take a good tablespoon of the mixture and form into balls, then roll in the chocolate shot. Place on trays lined with wax paper to harden overnight in the refrigerator. Put them into tins and refrigerate. If keeping for more than 4 weeks, they should be frozen. Take them out of the refrigerator a few hours before serving to soften slightly and bring out the rum flavour.

PREPARATION TIME: 15 minutes

DIANE'S SECRETS

The secret ingredient in my rum balls is the almond paste. In the early sixties, I decided to add to my family rum ball recipe some almond paste left over from my fruitcakes. It gave the rum balls a creamy texture and fabulous flavour. As well, I add lots of rum! Be sure to use the pure chocolate shot for coating the rum balls, as the artificial sprinkles are tasteless. The rum balls can also be rolled in Dutch cocoa for variety.

The Gourmet

Soups

Seventies

The Gourmet Seventies

THE SIXTIES MARKED THE DEBUT OF COMMERCIAL PACKAGED AND CANNED FOODS, which are still prominent on our grocery shelves today. But it was also the decade when exotic international foods startied to appear on grocers' shelves, and produce was fresher and more abundant. This lead to the seventies, the culinary decade that opened the door to learning the basics of French cuisine and to exploring the cooking techniques and specific ingredients of other global cooking traditions. With the debut of live television cooking shows and more cookbooks and cooking magazines being published, the food scene in the seventies was exploratory and dramatic. The buzzword was "gourmet"! Processed cheese slices or cheese spread on white bread was out: "croque-monsieur" sandwiches (something every French bistro would have on their menu) with Gruyère cheese and lean ham on French bread were in.

At the same time, ethnic restaurants were branching out of family neighbour-hoods into the mainstream of city dining establishments. Food and travel maga-zines were promoting vacations to foreign countries as global travel became more affordable for families. Our own family travelled a lot during that period, both overseas and in the United States and Canada. In 1971, Doug and I, and our children, Jennifer and Rand, toured Europe with our Richmond Kajaks track and field team, where our athletes competed in numerous competitions. In 1975 our children joined us once again to enjoy the Pan American Games in Mexico City, and in 1976 we loaded our Volkswagen van and drove across Canada to the Montreal Olympic Games, where Doug and I were both involved as officials. Once the Olympic Games were over, we travelled throughout the Maritimes. We then made our way home via the United States to end an unforgettable two months of travel.

It was fun for our family to experience the numerous ethnic cuisines and cultures as we travelled the world. It was also exciting for me to observe and learn from international chefs and to cook with them in their professional kitchens. The five-star chefs that made the greatest impact on the culinary world in the seventies, particularly in North America, and certainly on my own cooking career, were Julia Child, Michel Guérard, Anne Willan, Jacques Pépin and James Beard. They rocketed to international fame during the seventies and continue to inspire both professional and amateur chefs today.

Stepping into international kitchens and watching the chefs prepare our team meals was a great opportunity for me, a self-taught cook. Back in the fifties, when I first became interested in cooking, there were no professional schools solely dedicated to this vocation. It was a career dominated mainly by European male chefs who apprenticed at an early age in hotels or family restaurants. Women were not welcome and most male chefs, frankly, felt that the place for women to cook was in their own homes. Even today, this attitude still exists to some extent in European establishments, but gradually, women chefs worldwide are receiving the recognition and status they deserve. By the seventies, cooking schools such as the prestigious Cordon Bleu in London and Paris welcomed both men and women. As well, cooking schools were opening throughout Europe and the United States for both amateur and professional chefs.

Over the past five decades, I have had the privilege to continue to learn from chefs all over the world, either at our team's training camps or when attending cooking classes. In New York, San Francisco, Santa Fe, Paris, London, Italy, New Zealand and Australia, I've been fortunate to witness the passion and creativity of many talented chefs. So, in 1972, I was ready to open my cooking school back home in Richmond, British Columbia. My school, Entertaining With Diane Clement, was my effort to share my international cooking experiences and to bring the global cuisines into a teaching kitchen. It was one of the first cooking schools for amateur cooks in British Columbia.

Barry Downs, the award-winning West Coast architect, designed our new home with the cooking school in mind. The open family and cooking school kitchen setting was ideal for teaching the classes. I sent out the announcements of the school's opening, a little nervous and not knowing if there would be any interest or not. But the response was overwhelming. We had space for about 25, and we ended up squeezing in 30! The classes included an eight-week package, with one class per week, from 9:30 a.m. to 2:30 p.m. They included a cooking demonstration, based on a full menu, lunch with wines, along with all the recipes – all for $75! Even today, I meet former students who exclaim, "Diane, those classes were the food bargain of a lifetime!"

The cooking classes proved to be a valuable experience for everyone. It was hard work preparing for the classes, but the positive feedback was so encouraging for me, realizing that everyone went home with new recipes for entertaining and for everyday family meals. So many students were fearful of entertaining their partner's clients, or even friends, but by watching the menu being prepared, tasting it, and seeing the table settings, they gained the confidence they needed.

The "happy hour" in the seventies was the "in thing." The drinks usually included Scotch and rum, and the hot new wines had to include a Sauterne, Chablis or Reisling. Australian wines were making their debut with Lindemans leading the way with their Chardonnay. Mixed drinks were chic, with concoctions such as Kremlin Colonel, Party Girl Cocktail, Reform and Purple Cow. Grand Marnier, crème de menthe and brandies were the top three liqueurs, and coffees might include Café Brulot. Today, wines have replaced the hard liquor and liqueurs, but I just had to include two of the best punches of the seventies, Paddy's Punch and Frozen Rum Daiquiris. The first is to celebrate the "luck of the Irish" and the other is just to celebrate!

My family loved the school, too. Doug enjoyed the leftovers and Jennifer and Rand became familiar with exotic flavours at a very young age. They were always eager to taste the new surprises when I was taste testing my recipes.

Appetizers played a major role at dinner parties in the seventies. Often, we over-indulged in all the appetizers, saving no room for the main course. Four or five different nibbles were common, such as cheese trays, chafing dish meatballs, antipasto platters including prosciutto, marinated artichoke hearts and olive-stuffed eggs. Quiche Lorraine Tartlets (page 72) were popular then – and are still! In fact, Le Crocodile Restaurant, one of Vancouver's finest, serves them as their signature hors d'oeuvre, and they are awesome! ✃

Soon my students and I were ready for a new challenge. One morning in the fall of 1977, I asked my cooking class, "How would you like to spend Easter in Paris, to participate in the first bilingual school to offer a complete program in classic French cooking?" The school was L'École de Cuisine la Varenne. Situated on the fashionable Left Bank of Paris and backed by renowned chefs and authorities on French cuisine including Julia Child, Simone Beck and James Beard, La Varenne promoted itself as a school "for anyone who loves to cook, or wants to love to cook." Most of La Varenne's French chefs started their apprenticeship at the age of 12; some had worked as chefs at Maxim's in both Paris and Chicago and others had experience in numerous embassies.

I'd booked the school exclusively for seven days for 35 students, and the trip sold out immediately. The cost was unbelievable: airfare, eight-night accommodation at a four-star hotel including continental breakfasts, and a week's cooking course at La Varenne, all for $1,095! Our friends, Lily and Ken Richardson and their daughter, Theo, put this amazing package together for us through their travel agency. Lily attended most of my classes, loved to cook and entertain and was keen on being part of a "once-in-a-lifetime" cooking experience. So in April 1978, 35 excited women waved goodbye to their families for an Easter in Paris they would never forget!

When we arrived at La Varenne, the chefs were pleased to hear that we all loved to cook and that most of us had a good grasp of French cuisine. Little did they know, however, what they were in for! I'm sure La Varenne had never experienced such an outrageously enthusiastic group of students like our Vancouver contingent! We whipped around the fabulous kitchens creating what we thought were masterpiece dishes to impress the chefs. From the elegant Mushroom Seafood Pie à la Varenne (page 94) to a version of Julia Child's Gâteau au Chocolat (page 108), we learned how to prepare many mouthwatering dishes – and they're all included in this chapter for you to enjoy!

Although I didn't realize it at the time, the seventies marked the establishment of my two careers as an international sports official and as a chef/restaurateur and cookbook author. So I salute the seventies by sharing with you some of my favourite recipes from that time that have become my classics. I hope you will enjoy reliving this gourmet decade with me.

PADDY'S PUNCH

This punch has everyone dancing the Irish Jig, and it is to be served only on St. Paddy's Day. Green food colouring is optional!

INGREDIENTS
1 gallon medium dry sherry
1 bottle sweet vermouth
1 bottle gin
3 cups orange juice, fresh or canned
3 cups grapefruit juice, fresh or canned

METHOD
Blend all ingredients and chill. Serve with lots of ice.

PREPARATION TIME: 10 minutes

Gerry Gartside, founder of our Gourmet 8 luncheon group in 1969, decided to host her 1972 luncheon on St. Patrick's Day. I was her co-host. We wanted to make it extra special because the food editor of the Vancouver Sun and a photographer were to join us. We had just launched our second Gourmet 8 cookbook to rave reviews, and the paper was planning a feature on it and the authors: Gerry Gartside, Sheila Dixon, Wendy MacSorley, Wilma Dixon, Ann Gibb, Barbara Vance, Billie Meadows and me.

Martha Stewart's tips on entertaining wouldn't surface until the eighties, so we were left to our own imaginations to create our party themes. Sometimes we went overboard, and our St. Patrick's Day Buffet was definitely one of those times! Our menu was festive with Paddy's Punch, Belfast Steak and Kidney Stew, Colcannon Casserole, Irish Soda Bread, Shamrock Salad, Emerald Isle Mallow and, naturally, Irish Coffee. Everything was green and white and lots of little leprechauns decorated the table. Even the food was tinted green, and when the Sun photographer asked us all to smile for a picture in front of the buffet, he started to laugh because our tongues were green from the colouring in the punch. Thank heaven the picture was in black and white! ⚘

FROZEN RUM DAIQUIRIS

This rum punch can be made ahead and will keep for weeks in the freezer. It's a refreshing drink to have on hand for summertime entertaining.

INGREDIENTS
1 bottle (25 oz) white rum
1 tin (12½ oz) frozen limeade concentrate
4 cups lemon-lime carbonated beverage
   (Sprite or 7-Up)
¾ cup water

METHOD
At least two days before serving, combine all ingredients and freeze in airtight container.

Twenty minutes before serving, transfer to a punch bowl and stir until smooth and mushy. Pour into small goblets. Garnish each with a thin slice of lime.

PREPARATION TIME: 10 minutes

JAMES BEARD'S CRUDITÉS, CIRCA 1974

This tomato teaser from James Beard is the conversation piece of any party. When we hosted our expansion party at our Tomato Fresh Food Café, we had these crudités circulating and Malcolm Parry, the dynamic social columnist for the *Vancouver Sun*, named them "The Tomato Tomatini"!

Start your party by distributing the vodka, tomatoes and salt in martini glasses throughout the house (living room, hallways, family room) to tease your guests' palates. They'll be the hit of the party.

PROVIDE FOR YOUR GUESTS
A bowl of very small cherry tomatoes (use the
    yellow variety as well, if available)
Small wooden skewers
Vodka glass ¾ full of vodka
Vodka glass ¾ full of French coarse crystal sea salt

METHOD
Dip the cherry tomatoes in the vodka for a "martini punch," then into the sea salt for a "salty crunch." If you pierce the tomatoes with the skewers before dipping them into the vodka, you'll get a bigger punch!

PREPARATION TIME: 10 minutes

In January 1985, my sister-in-law, Dianne Matheson, and I were attending cooking classes in New York at Lydie Marshall's La Bonne Cocotte in Greenwich Village. James Beard was Lydie's neighbour and longtime friend, and he loved to drop by the cooking classes to enjoy the food prepared by her students.

One afternoon, Dianne and I were shopping at New York's famous Zabar's Deli when a camera crew approached us and asked what we thought of the news of James Beard's death that morning at the age of 86. Zabar's was Beard's favourite deli, and all the staff were in shock on hearing the news. Dianne and I were sure Lydie would cancel our classes that evening, but she decided to proceed, telling us, "James wouldn't have wanted it any other way."

As we prepared our dishes, she related many warm stories of one of the world's most creative and passionate chefs. His cookbooks were an inspiration to all cooks in the early seventies, and I still refer to them today. He had flare and style, and he made complicated dishes simple.

Today, the James Beard Foundation has been established in his home in Greenwich Village, with a teaching kitchen and library. It's a non-profit foundation, founded by Julia Child, for the "preservation of Beard's tradition, remembering America's past and promoting its future." Today, many of our British Columbian chefs have been part of the culinary teams presenting fundraising dinners in New York for the James Beard Foundation. ✀

QUICHE LORRAINE TARTLETS

MAKES ABOUT 24

Throughout the seventies, these miniature quiches appeared at every cocktail party, family celebration, and festive occasion. Sometimes they were made into larger tarts as a main entrée. My friend, Barbara Watts, has been my assistant and coordinator for many of my cooking classes over the past three decades. Barbara and I have made tons of quiches for our classes and numerous receptions.

Barb was the one who convinced me to teach cooking classes in the early seventies at the newly opened YWCA in Vancouver, which turned out to be the start of my cooking career. More recently, she has been an assistant for Julia Child in numerous cooking demonstrations in the United States, raising funds for the culinary and hospitality related professions. Barbara is always there for me, and I cherish her friendship. This recipe is dedicated to her.

INGREDIENTS

PASTRY
½ cup shortening
1 ⅓ cups all-purpose flour
¼ cup ice water

FILLING
6 slices bacon
2 large eggs
1 cup whipping cream
½ tsp salt
1 tsp sugar
Pinch nutmeg
Pinch pepper
½ cup shredded Swiss or Gruyère cheese

METHOD

PASTRY

In a medium-size bowl, cut shortening into flour until the mixture resembles small peas. Sprinkle ice water over the mixture, a tablespoon at a time, tossing with a fork until all particles are moistened. Form into a ball. Chill in refrigerator for about 15 minutes. Roll out about ¼-inch thick on a lightly floured surface; cut into 2-inch circles. Fit each circle into 24 small tart pans, 1¾-inch size.

FILLING

Heat oven to 400°F. Fry the bacon until crisp; pat dry and crumble. Combine the eggs, whipping cream, salt, sugar, nutmeg and pepper. Beat to blend well. Sprinkle each tart shell with bacon, then cheese. Fill each cup with egg mixture being careful not to overflow. Bake for 12 to 15 minutes or until the pastry is golden. Reduce heat to 350°F and bake for 10 minutes longer or until the filling is firm. Do not overbake. Cool, remove from pans, freeze, or store in the refrigerator for up to 2 days ahead of serving.

To serve, thaw if frozen. Reheat for about 10 minutes at 325°F or until heated through.

PREPARATION TIME: 40 minutes

DIANE'S SECRETS

These tartlets freeze beautifully. Double the filling and you have the makings of a traditional quiche, cooked in an 8- or 9-inch pie shell.

GUACAMOLE

Serve this with Tortilla Pie (page 88) and lots of corn chips, or by itself with the chips as an appetizer. This version of the ever-popular guacamole is made smoother by the addition of sour cream.

Less fat: Use low-fat sour cream or eliminate it completely.

INGREDIENTS
4 to 5 medium ripe avocados, peeled and mashed
1 to 2 tsp chili powder, to taste
1 to 2 tsp white vinegar, to taste
1 tbsp lemon juice
3 tbsp green onion, finely chopped
2 small tomatoes, diced
1 cup sour cream
Salt and pepper to taste

METHOD
About an hour before serving, combine all ingredients, reserving about ½ cup of the sour cream. Spread the reserved sour cream in an even layer on top of the guacamole to prevent the mixture from turning brown. Seal and refrigerate.

Just before serving, blend in the sour cream topping. Adjust seasonings to taste.

PREPARATION TIME: 10 minutes

SHAMROCK SALAD

Jellied salads were as popular as ever in the seventies. This one was on the St. Patrick's Day menu for my cooking club, the Gourmet 8, back in 1972, along with Irish Stew (page 86). It can be made a day ahead.

INGREDIENTS
2 packages (3-oz size) lime jelly powder
1 tbsp lemon juice
2 tbsp white vinegar
2 tsp onion, grated
Salt and pepper to taste
1 cup mayonnaise
2 cups sour cream
1 English cucumber, finely chopped

GARNISH
½ English cucumber, thinly sliced

METHOD
Prepare the first layer by dissolving 1 package of jelly powder in 1 cup boiling water with the lemon juice added. Pour into a 6-cup oiled jelly mould; chill until partially set.

Prepare the second layer by dissolving the second package of jelly powder in 2 cups of boiling water. Stir in the vinegar, onion, salt and pepper. Chill until partially set. Blend in the mayonnaise and sour cream. Fold in the chopped cucumbers, which have been patted dry with paper towels.

Spoon the mayonnaise mixture on top of the first layer in the salad mould, spreading evenly. Chill until firm.

To serve, unmould onto a salad plate. Decorate with slices of cucumbers around the mould.

PREPARATION TIME: 30 minutes

SHARON'S CAESAR SALAD

Sharon and John Woyat and their family have shared many family gatherings with our Clement clan. Sharon's quick Caesar dressing is sensational. Food critic, cookbook author and television personality Jurgen Gothe exclaims: "This caesar dressing and the heavy parmesan and garlic croutons remain my staple!" We served it from day one at our Tomato Café to rave reviews. One customer liked it so much he devoured a large Caesar, then ordered another one "to go," to eat on his plane trip to Toronto! Try it with our Grilled Chicken with Red Pepper Chutney (page 148), another popular choice at the Tomato.

INGREDIENTS
2 large heads romaine lettuce,
    torn into bite-size pieces
Fresh grated Parmesan cheese

DRESSING
2 large eggs
6 tbsp lemon juice
Pepper to taste
1 large clove garlic, minced
½ cup Parmesan cheese, freshly grated
1 can (3½ oz) anchovies, including oil
½ cup olive oil, or a blend of olive and salad oil

CROUTONS
4 to 6 cups sourdough bread, cut into small cubes
4 to 6 large cloves garlic, crushed (optional)
1 cup grated Parmesan cheese
½ cup olive oil, or a blend of olive and salad oil

METHOD

Prepare dressing and croutons. In a large bowl, pour enough dressing over lettuce to coat. Sprinkle with croutons and Parmesan cheese; toss.

DRESSING

In a food processor, blend together eggs, lemon juice, pepper, garlic, Parmesan cheese and anchovies. Pour in the oil slowly until thickened to a smooth, creamy consistency.

CROUTONS

Heat oven to 300°F. In a large bowl, toss the bread cubes with the garlic and Parmesan cheese. Drizzle enough of the oil over top to just coat the cubes. Toss. Bake for 40 to 45 minutes, stirring the cubes after 20 minutes, until they are golden, crisp and dry. They should be crunchy to the taste. Cool. (May be stored in the refrigerator for weeks.)

PREPARATION TIME: 50 minutes, including baking croutons

DIANE'S SECRETS

My pet peeve is limp romaine. Make sure you pat your lettuce dry and store by layering with paper towels in a plastic container. It should keep several days in the refrigerator. Take the time to make your own croutons with this recipe. The boxed commercial varieties with their artificial flavours just aren't the same!

ASPARAGUS NIÇOISE

SERVES 6

In 1994, while staying at Eileen and Paul Dwillies' delightful village home in southern France, we made a habit of wandering down to the local Sunday farmer's market in the village of Nyon to select the ingredients for our evening meal. One day, taking time for lunch, we chose this light and refreshing asparagus salad at one of the family bistros. Here is my interpretation.

INGREDIENTS
2 lbs fresh thick asparagus, trimmed
2 tomatoes, peeled, seeded and finely chopped
½ cup niçoise or calamata olives, rinsed,
  pitted if desired
2 tbsp capers

DRESSING
3 tbsp red wine vinegar
2 tsp Dijon mustard
⅔ cup olive oil
Salt and pepper to taste

METHOD
Blanche the asparagus in a boiling water for about 3 minutes, or until *al dente*. Put in an ice water bath to cool immediately. Pat dry.

On your serving platter, arrange the asparagus spears. Over top, sprinkle the tomatoes, niçoise olives and capers. Drizzle the dressing evenly over the salad to coat lightly. Sprinkle a little pepper over all.

DRESSING
Blend the red wine vinegar with the Dijon mustard. Slowly whisk in the olive oil. Salt and pepper to taste.

PREPARATION TIME: 15 minutes

DIANE'S SECRETS

You can prepare the asparagus a day ahead, layering the spears on a plate lined with paper towels to soak up any moisture. Cover with plastic wrap and refrigerate until ready to serve. It is worth the time to peel the tips of the asparagus before blanching for a truly elegant presentation. The dressing may also be made a day or two ahead and refrigerated.

Double the dressing recipe if you wish to pass to guests at the table, should they want more.

In the seventies, Michel Guérard, one of France's most celebrated chefs, announced the debut of his "nouvelle cuisine," or "cuisine minceur" as he liked to call it. This low-fat style of French cooking challenged Julia Child's rich, classic French cuisine. Guérard proclaimed to the world: "This is the revolutionary way to cook beautiful French food without the calories!" He made world headlines, and was touted as France's true pioneer of low-fat, high-pleasure cuisine. He received three stars, the highest honour, from the respected Michelin Guide for his famous spa and restaurant in the Basque countryside. Chef Guérard was one of the few chefs in the world at that time to receive such a tribute.

But why this move toward healthier cuisine? The story goes that Chef Guérard became so rotund from all the butters and cream he used that Christine, the love of his life, gave him an ultimatum to "lose weight, or the romance is over." Rather than lose his treasured Christine, he developed the new style, now commonly known as "spa cuisine" in North America.

Chefs around the world soon began creating Michel Guérard's nouvelle cuisine for their patrons. They flocked to his spa and restaurant to learn his new recipes and healthy approach. Some, however, took it to the extreme and their sparse plate presentations were not praised by their patrons.

Over the decades, we have come to recognize that it is important to eat a healthy diet but still maintain balance and choice. We all know we can't eat Christmas dinner every day, but a splurge now and then on special occasions should not make anyone feel guilty. Julia Child and Michel Guérard both made great contributions to cuisine in the seventies, one simplifying classic French cooking, and one making us aware that we can still enjoy the classics, but with a little healthier approach. ॐ

DAPHNE FRANCIS' CREAM OF TOMATO SOUP

I have enjoyed serving on the Board of Directors for the Vancouver International Film Festival for more than a decade. Our chairman, Michael Francis, has always raved about his wife Daphne's fabulous tomato soup, which she adapted from one of James Beard's original recipes. Daphne, who chaired the British Columbia UNICEF organization for years and is active on many Vancouver charity fundraisers, entertains frequently, and this soup is one of her most requested recipes. It's rich, sinful, and should be served only in small portions for special celebration dinners. The fresh tomatoes are the key, and the brandy, of course!

INGREDIENTS
1 small onion, finely chopped
3 tbsp unsalted butter
1/4 tsp baking soda
6 large, ripe tomatoes, peeled, seeded and
    coarsely chopped
2 tbsp fresh basil
1/2 cup whipping cream
1 1/2 cups whole milk
Pinch salt and pepper
1 to 2 tbsp brandy (optional)
1 tbsp sour cream (optional)

METHOD

In a medium-size saucepan, sauté the onion in butter until soft and golden. Add the baking soda and tomatoes. Cook for 10 to 12 minutes, or until thickened and paste-like. Remove from heat and stir in the basil, whipping cream, milk, salt and pepper. Taste and adjust seasonings as desired.

Pour into small soup bowls. Add a dash of brandy to each bowl, and top with sour cream if desired.

PREPARATION TIME: 30 minutes

Less fat: Substitute 2 cups whole milk for the milk and whipping cream. Top with low-fat yogurt instead of sour cream.

DIANE'S SECRETS

This soup can be refrigerated a day ahead and reheated when ready to serve. If it has become too thick during refrigeration, just add a little more milk as you reheat.

COLCANNON CASSEROLE

SERVES 8

This traditional Irish potato, parsnip and cabbage vegetable dish boasts a soufflé topping and is the perfect marriage to the gutsy Irish Stew (page 86). It can be prepared a day ahead, except for the last stage of adding the topping.

INGREDIENTS
4 large potatoes
2 parsnips
1 cup cooked green cabbage, chopped
2 onions, finely chopped
⅔ cup whole milk
Salt and pepper to taste
2 egg whites
½ cup grated Cheddar cheese
¼ cup chopped parsley

METHOD

Cook the potatoes and parsnips together in boiling water until tender. Drain and mash. In another pot, cook the cabbage in boiling water about 10 minutes or until tender. Drain; add to the potatoes and parsnips.

Cook the onions in the milk until soft. Add to the other vegetables and season with salt and pepper. Mix thoroughly. (Can be prepared up to this point and refrigerated for up to a day.)

Beat egg whites until stiff. Fold the cheese into the egg whites and spread evenly on top of casserole. Bake at 350°F for 35 to 40 minutes until hot and golden. Sprinkle with chopped parsley and serve.

PREPARATION TIME: 30 minutes

DIANE'S TOMATO CHEESE ONION PESTO SANDWICH (TCOP)

SERVES 1

In the seventies, thick grilled cheese sandwiches loaded with tomatoes, tuna, bacon or turkey – you name it – were on every menu. From tuna melts to double cheese and bacon, we couldn't get enough of them. Try this wonderful open-face tomato, cheese, onion and pesto combination, lovingly known as the TCOP at the Tomato Café.

INGREDIENTS
2 (½-inch) slices of French bread, toasted
4 tbsp pesto mayonnaise (see Diane's secrets, below)
⅓ cup grated Danish fontina cheese
6 tomato slices
2 sun-dried tomatoes, softened and chopped
A few paper-thin slices of red onions

METHOD
Place the toasted bread slices on a cookie sheet. On each piece of toast, spread a layer of the pesto mayonnaise, saving some for the topping. Divide the cheese evenly over both slices of toast. Grill until the cheese is melted, about 2 to 3 minutes. Top each piece with 3 overlapping tomato slices, a little pesto mayonnaise and the sun-dried tomatoes. Sprinkle onions over each piece and serve immediately.

PREPARATION TIME: 10 minutes

 DIANE'S SECRETS *For a quick pesto mayonnaise, blend 2 to 3 tbsp of commercial pesto with a cup of mayonnaise. As a variation, you can pop the tomatoes under the grill to heat slightly before adding the pesto mayonnaise and sun-dried tomatoes on top.*

My regular cravings for a thick, cheesy tomato sandwich led to the decision to put the TCOP on the menu when we opened the Tomato Café. We described it as "tomatoes, fontina cheese, onion and pesto, open and facing you," waiting to be devoured. From time to time my partners, Jennifer and Christian along with the head chef, review our menus to add or subtract an item. It seems that whenever we are considering removing the TCOP, that very week we get lots of requests for it! I grin to myself and declare, "The TCOP stays! It's a total comfort sandwich." There's nothing more soothing on a cold rainy day.

Less fat: Use low-fat cheese and mayonnaise.

EGGS BENNY IN A VOLKSWAGEN

In 1976, Doug and I decided that rather than fly to Montreal for the Olympic Games, we would drive across Canada in our own Volkswagen camper van with our children, Jennifer and Rand. Once in a while, on the road, we all had a craving for eggs Benedict. Rather than taking the time to stop in a busy restaurant, I would whip up my super-quick version, which has become my family's favourite. It worked well, even in the little Volkswagen's makeshift kitchen. The mock hollandaise sauce is foolproof. And I'll let you in on a little secret: we use it for our eggs Benny dishes at the Tomato Café!

INGREDIENTS
1 ½ cups mayonnaise
½ cup sour cream
1 tbsp lemon juice
1 tsp Dijon mustard
Salt and pepper to taste
1 tsp vinegar
8 eggs
Pinch salt
24 slices European back bacon
4 English muffins, split in half
Paprika (optional)
1 tomato, sliced

METHOD
In a saucepan, combine mayonnaise, sour cream, lemon juice, mustard, salt and pepper. Keep warm over low heat in a double boiler. Do not overheat.

TO POACH THE EGGS
Fill a large, shallow pan with about 3 inches of water. Bring to a low boil, add a pinch of salt and the vinegar. Crack the eggs separately in a small bowl and gently drop into the water. Simmer eggs 2 at a time to avoid breaking yolks, 3 to 5 minutes, depending on how firm you like your eggs. Place on paper towels while you poach the remaining eggs. When ready to serve, reheat eggs in a little hot water for about 1 minute.

Fry the bacon slices and toast the muffins. Top each muffin half with bacon slices and egg. Spoon hot sauce over top. Sprinkle with paprika and serve with tomato slices.

PREPARATION TIME: 15 minutes

DIANE'S SECRETS

Be very careful when heating the sauce. If it gets too hot, it will curdle. You can keep it warm on top of a double boiler to prevent overheating. Be sure to use real mayonnaise in this recipe; I like Hellman's or Kraft. I also often offer a choice of either smoked salmon, spinach or fresh asparagus as an alternative to the bacon.

In 1972, Doug and I had decided not to attend the Munich Games, and we excitedly watched on television as our Canadian athletes competed. That excitement changed to shock and disbelief when Israeli Olympic team members were taken hostage by a Palestinian terrorist organization. Later, 11 team members were murdered. As we mourned the loss of these honourable Olympians, we asked ourselves, "Could the Olympic Games ever be the same again?"

Four years later, the 1976 Olympic Games were held in Montreal. It was an honour for me, as President of the Canadian Track and Field Association, and the first woman president of an Olympic National Sports Federation in the world, to host my international athletics family. At the same time, Doug was the athletic team physician and middle distance coach. After what happened in Munich, the Olympics took on a very different atmosphere. The security costs for each athlete and official at the 1976 Olympics were $8,000 per head. But the organizing committee hosted a safe and outstanding Games. Princess Anne, representing Great Britain in the equestrian events, mingled freely with other Olympians in the athletes' village. The evening of the opening ceremonies, our great Canadian folksinger Gordon Lightfoot performed in the athletes' outdoor concert stage. It was a magical evening under the stars, with athletes from over 160 countries singing along and relaxing before their competition commenced. The true spirit of the Olympic Games returned that evening and throughout the Games! &

IRISH STEW

This particular Irish Stew boasts the addition of oysters, kidneys, sherry and mushrooms. Serve it with Calconnon Casserole (page 82).

INGREDIENTS
1 large beef kidney
1½ lb chuck or round beef steak
3 tbsp flour
Pinch cayenne
Salt and pepper to taste
½ tsp mace
3 tbsp butter
1 large onion, finely chopped
2 strips bacon, finely chopped
½ lb fresh mushrooms, thinly sliced
3 cups beef stock or water
1 bay leaf
½ pint oysters
3 tbsp dry sherry
¼ cup chopped parsley

METHOD

Remove tissue from the kidney; soak in lightly salted water for about 2 hours. Cut into small pieces with scissors. Cut the steak into 1½ inch cubes. Combine the flour, cayenne, salt, pepper and mace in a plastic bag. Add the kidney and beef and shake to coat lightly. Set aside.

Melt the butter in a fry pan. Add the onion, bacon and mushrooms and sauté until golden. Transfer to a medium-size casserole and set aside.

Sauté the kidney and steak a few minutes until browned, adding a little more butter if necessary. Add the kidney and beef to the casserole, stirring to blend. Cover all with the stock and add the bay leaf. Bake at 350°F for 1½ to 2 hours or until beef is tender. Stir frequently during cooking. Remove bay leaf. (Can be cooled and refrigerated at this point up to a day ahead of serving. Reheat at 325°F for 35 to 40 minutes or until hot.)

Add oysters and bake for 10 more minutes or until the oysters are cooked. Stir in the sherry and sprinkle with parsley.

PREPARATION TIME: 20 minutes

TORTILLA PIE

SERVES 8

In 1975 Doug and I were in Mexico City for the Pan American Games. Doug and our friend Peter Webster from Vancouver were part of the managerial staff for the Canadian team. Our children, Jennifer and Rand, and our friend Devine Elden joined us as well for two weeks of sightseeing, excellent competition, spectacular opening and closing ceremonies and the best of Mexican cuisine.

This Mexican version of Italian lasagna, with layers of corn tortillas, ground beef, creamy cheese and a spicy tomato sauce reminds me of the many similar dishes we tasted in the festive Mexican restaurants. It's been my standby whenever athletes drop by for an impromptu meal after a workout.

INGREDIENTS
1 tbsp vegetable oil
1 ½ lb lean ground beef
1 onion, finely chopped
2 cloves garlic, crushed
½ cup Heinz chili sauce
   (see Diane's secrets, page 19)
2 cans (28-oz size) chopped tomatoes
1 cup mild taco sauce
Pinch cinnamon
Pepper to taste
2 cans (4-oz size) chopped mild chilies
18 (6-in size) corn tortillas
8 cups grated Monterey Jack cheese
Sour cream
½ cup finely chopped green onions

METHOD

In a large fry pan, heat the oil and sauté the beef until brown. Drain well, reserving 2 tbsp of the fat. Set the beef aside.

Sauté the onion and garlic in the reserved fat until the onions are softened slightly. Add the chili sauce, tomatoes, taco sauce, cinnamon, pepper and cooked beef. Bring to a boil and simmer for 30 minutes, stirring often. Add the chilies and stir. Cool.

In a large lasagna-type pan (13x9 inches), layer 6 tortillas, one-third of the tomato sauce mixture, and one-third of the cheese. Repeat layers, ending with sauce and cheese. Pat down well. (You can prepare ahead to this point, then refrigerate the dish covered until ready to cook.)

Bake at 350°F for 30 to 40 minutes or until hot and bubbly. Just before serving, spoon some sour cream in a strip down the middle of the casserole and sprinkle with the green onions. Serve with additional sour cream and onions on the side.

PREPARATION TIME: 45 minutes

Less fat: Be sure to use lean beef and to drain off the fat well. You can also reduce the amount of cheese and sour cream used, and use low-fat varieties.

DIANE'S SECRETS

This is the perfect family casserole for home, après-ski – whenever. Add lots of guacamole, salsa, corn chips, refried beans and chilled Mexican beer and you have a party!

KASEY WILSON'S LAMB MARRAKECH

SERVES 6 TO 8

Kasey is one of Canada's premier food, wine and travel writers, restaurant reviewer, author of several cookbooks, editor of *Vancouver Best Places,* and co-editor of *The Pacific Northwest Zagat Restaurant Survey.* As well, she co-hosts the Vancouver CFUN radio show "The Best of Food and Wine" with wine expert Anthony Gismondi. Besides all that, she has been a dear friend and colleague for almost 30 years. She loves food as much as I do, and she was one of the first to sign up for my cooking classes and to join us at La Varenne, in Paris in 1978, along with her twin sister.

This signature lamb dish of Kasey's is a perfect buffet dish. I frequently serve it at my dinner parties, and it's one of my all-time favourites. Kasey suggests that the flavour of the lamb Marrakech improves when it's refrigerated overnight.

INGREDIENTS
3 lb lean boneless lamb shoulder, cut into
    ½-inch thick slices
¼ cup peanut or vegetable oil
2 large onions, finely chopped
4 cloves garlic, chopped
½ tsp salt
¼ tsp crushed red pepper flakes, or to taste
1 tbsp Spice Parisienne (see below)
1 tsp turmeric
3 large tomatoes, peeled, seeded and chopped
    or 1 can (28 oz) plum tomatoes, chopped
1 cup raisins, soaked in sherry just to cover
1 cup toasted cashews, almonds or peanuts
    (see Diane's secrets, next page)

METHOD

In a large, heavy saucepan over medium-high heat, brown the lamb in oil for about 5 minutes. Add the onions and garlic and brown lightly. Add remaining ingredients, except for the nuts. Blend all ingredients well and simmer for a few minutes, stirring constantly.

Remove from stove, cover pan and bake in a 350°F oven for 1½ hours or until the lamb is tender. (Can be made ahead to this point and refrigerated overnight. Reheat, covered, in a 350°F oven for 35 to 40 minutes or until hot.) Add the nuts just before serving.

KASEY'S SPICE PARISIENNE

MAKES ABOUT ¼ CUP

Spice Parisienne is a unique blend of spices and herbs patterned after a continental formula that has long been a favourite of European and Scandinavian chefs. It is interchangeable with pepper and may be used in dips, soups, sauces, pâtés and meatballs, among other foods.

In a blender or food processor, blend together 1 tsp ground cinnamon, 2 tsp ground allspice, ¾ tsp ground cloves, ¾ tsp ground nutmeg, 2 tsp tarragon (optional), 2 tsp dried thyme leaves and 2 tsp ground coriander.

PREPARATION TIME: 30 minutes

DIANE'S SECRETS

To toast nuts or seeds, just spread on a cookie sheet and roast at 350°F for 5 to 7 minutes. Check frequently to prevent overbrowning.

CHICKEN CACCIATORE

Throughout the seventies, this glorified Italian chicken and stewed tomato dish became our Saturday night standby. Often, several athletes would end up at our house after a track and field meet and join us for dinner, so I was always prepared with a hearty post-race dinner. Along with the Cacciatore, I always added "oodles of noodles" or rice, a huge salad, hearty breads, Italian wine and something chocolate. For a superb chocolate finish to this meal, try Jane's Chocolate Pound Cake (page 160).

INGREDIENTS
3 tbsp olive oil
4 cloves garlic, chopped
2 large onions, sliced, about 2 cups
½ lb mushrooms, sliced
3 celery stalks, thinly sliced on the diagonal
2 large carrots, peeled and thinly sliced
1 cup dry red wine
Salt and pepper to taste
1 tbsp fresh oregano, or 1 tsp dry
1 tbsp fresh thyme, or 1 tsp dry
3½ to 4 lb chicken, cut into serving-size pieces
1 can (28 oz) chopped tomatoes, with juice
¼ cup fresh parsley, chopped
Parmesan cheese, grated

METHOD

Heat the oil in a large fry pan or Dutch oven. Add the garlic, onions, mushrooms, celery and carrots and sauté several minutes until the onions and mushrooms soften. Add the red wine and simmer for about 5 minutes. Add salt, pepper, oregano and thyme. Transfer to a bowl and set aside while you prepare the chicken.

Heat a little more olive oil in the fry pan or Dutch oven and brown the chicken pieces until golden. Return the onion-mushroom mixture to the pan and add the tomatoes. Bring to a boil, reduce heat to medium, cover and simmer for about 30 minutes. Check the chicken breasts for doneness. When cooked, remove the breasts from the pan and set aside in the refrigerator.

Uncover the fry pan and simmer sauce 20 to 25 minutes or until the sauce is reduced and the remaining chicken pieces are very tender. Return the cooked chicken breasts to the pan and heat through. (Can be made ahead to this point and refrigerated overnight. To reheat, cover and place in a 350°F oven for 35 to 40 minutes or until heated through.)

Top with parsley and serve with noodles or rice. Pass the parmesan.

PREPARATION TIME: 1½ to 2 hours

DIANE'S SECRETS

I prefer to make this dish in the oven, rather than simmering on top of the stove. You don't have to keep watch over it as much and there is less risk of the sauce reducing too much. Follow the same directions for cooking as above but cook in a 350°F oven.

Always remember to use plastic wrap when covering and refrigerating any dish with tomatoes. Aluminum foil will react chemically with the acid in the tomatoes and cause the foil to break down and stick to the sauce. Always completely cool any tomato dish before covering to prevent it from souring.

MUSHROOM SEAFOOD PIE À LA VARENNE

SERVES 6

In 1979, I invited La Varenne founder, Anne Willan, to our home while she was visiting in Vancouver. Anne is married to Mark Cherviavsky, who was an executive with the World Bank at that time. Mark has family ties in Vancouver, and so they return to Vancouver from time to time. On this particular visit, I invited the media and my group of students who attended La Varenne to a luncheon in Anne's honour. I featured some of the outstanding specialties we created at her school, including the Mushroom Seafood Pie. French wines flowed freely!

This dish was voted one of the top five of those we prepared at La Varenne cooking school in Paris in April 1978, when I took my own students there for 10 days. When I returned home, my family asked me, "When are you going to serve us something from La Varenne?" A few days later, I surprised them with this recipe. It's a versatile dish that can be served as an appetizer or as a main dish, for a light luncheon or dinner. Make it the day ahead and reheat before serving.

INGREDIENTS

CRUST
2 cups all-purpose flour
½ tsp salt
1 cup plus 2 tbsp butter
2 egg yolks
6 tbsp ice cold water

FILLING
3 tbsp butter
½ onion, finely chopped
½ lb mushrooms
3 tbsp finely chopped shallots or green onions
3 tbsp all-purpose flour
1½ cups light cream or whole milk
Pinch nutmeg
Pinch salt and pepper
3 egg yolks, whisked slightly
¼ lb fresh crabmeat
¼ lb fresh shrimp
3 tbsp chopped parsley
1 egg
1 tbsp water

DIANE'S SECRETS

This dish can be cooked and refrigerated overnight. To serve, reheat in a 350°F oven for 35 minutes or until hot. For a change, I like to make this pie in an oblong flan pan and cut into squares as an appetizer or first course.

METHOD

CRUST

In a food processor: Combine flour and salt, then add butter, egg yolks and water. Mix to form a ball.

By hand: Mix together flour and salt. Cut in the butter. Combine egg yolks and water and add to flour mixture, mixing with a fork to form a soft ball.

Chill at least 30 minutes (or wrap and freeze for use later).

FILLING

Melt butter in a heavy saucepan, add onion and cook over medium heat until soft but not brown. Stir in the mushrooms and cook rapidly, stirring occasionally until all the moisture has evaporated. Do not overcook. Stir in the shallots or onions and continue cooking for about 1 minute longer. Stir in the flour, then the cream, nutmeg, salt and pepper. Cook, stirring, until the mixture thickens; simmer for about 2 minutes.

Remove the saucepan from the heat and beat the egg yolks gradually into the hot mixture. Fold in the crab, shrimp and parsley. Taste and adjust seasonings. Cool.

Heat over to 400°F. Roll out two-thirds of the dough to line a 9-inch pie pan or an 11x7½-inch pan. Prick the bottom lightly with a fork and chill. Spread the cooled filling in pie shell.

Roll out remaining dough and cut into thin strips. Lay a diagonal lattice over the filling, pressing the ends well down onto shell edge to seal. If necessary, cover the edge with a strip of dough to make it neat. Whisk together egg and water and brush over the lattice. Bake for 30 to 35 minutes until the pastry is brown and the filling starts to bubble.

VARIATION

For Mushroom Pie, substitute an additional ½ lb mushrooms for the shrimp and crabmeat.

PREPARATION TIME: 45 minutes

Anne Willan was born in England and graduated in Business from Cambridge. However, she also loved to cook, and she subsequently graduated from the prestigious Cordon Bleu Cooking School before opening her cooking school in Paris in 1975.

Over the decades, Anne has written many best-selling cookbooks, opened cooking schools in both France and the United States and has had her own television series. She has been my role model in the culinary profession. I've learned from her that patience is a definite virtue in this business, and that family support and a strong team in your workplace is crucial for success.

Less fat: Use whole milk, not light cream, and eliminate one of the egg yolks.

NASI GORENG WITH CONDIMENTS AND SIDE DISHES

The glamorous rijstaffel (pronounced rye-stefful) is Dutch for "rice table," and its origins are the exotic Spice Islands of Indonesia. A rijstaffel table might include over 35 exotic dishes, but a simpler rijstaffel is provided here, Nasi Goreng with a few condiments and side dishes to complement the rice specialty. This recipe is not too spicy; you can use more or less spice to suit your taste buds. Serve in large soup bowls with the rice in the middle, adding the condiments and side dishes around it.

NASI GORENG

SERVES 8

The rice dish can be made several hours or the day ahead and reheated before serving. The ham and egg strips can be prepared a few hours ahead and added to the rice casserole in the last 15 minutes of reheating.

INGREDIENTS

RICE DISH
3 cups uncooked long-grain white rice
2 cloves garlic, crushed
2 tbsp fresh ginger, peeled and finely chopped
1 tbsp turmeric
1 tbsp ground coriander
1½ tsp ground cumin
Pinch salt
6 cups chicken stock

HAM AND EGG STRIPS
1 tbsp olive oil
½ lb ham, sliced into ¼-inch strips
6 large eggs
Salt and pepper to taste
1 tbsp butter

METHOD

RICE DISH

In a greased 3-quart casserole, combine all rice dish ingredients except the chicken stock. Blend well. In a saucepan, bring the chicken stock to boiling and pour over the casserole mixture. Stir lightly to blend. Cover and bake in oven at 350°F for 50 minutes until cooked and the all the liquid has been absorbed. (If prepared ahead, reheat in oven at 350°F for 35 to 40 minutes or until heated through.)

HAM AND EGG STRIPS

In a fry pan, heat oil and sauté the ham strips a few minutes. Set aside. In a bowl, beat the eggs slightly; add salt and pepper to taste. In fry pan, melt the butter and add the eggs. Cook until set, like an omelette. Turn out on cutting board. Cut into large strips and set aside with the ham strips. Add the ham and egg strips to the rice dish for the last 15 minutes of cooking or reheating. Serve.

PREPARATION TIME: The beauty of the Rijstaffel is that it can be prepared a day ahead, which is a real treat to the host. Allow 2 to 3 hours to organize and make the various dishes and to set up your condiment bowls and platters.

RIJSTAFFEL CONDIMENTS

Provide 1½ to 2 cups of each condiment

TOASTED COCONUT

Spread desired amount of coconut on cookie sheet and toast in oven at 350°F for 10 minutes or until golden. Stir often, and be careful not to burn. Can be made days ahead and kept in sealed container. (Note: Toast 2 cups to allow extra for the chicken saté dish. See page 99.)

RAISINS

Soak desired amount of raisins in enough sherry to cover for 1 hour. Drain.

KRUPUKS

Krupuks, also known as Indonesian wafers or Chinese prawn-flavoured chips, can be found in gourmet sections of food stores. To cook, heat 1 inch vegetable oil in fry pan. Using kitchen tongs, dip each krupuk in hot oil, turning once. Drain on paper towels. Can be made several hours before serving and left at room temperature until ready to use.

CUCUMBERS IN YOGURT

In mixing bowl, combine 2 cups thinly sliced English cucumber patted dry on paper towel, 1 cup plain yogurt, 1 tbsp finely chopped green onion or chives, ½ tsp Madras curry powder, pinch each of salt and pepper, 1 tbsp sugar and juice of ½ lemon. Chill. Best made several hours before serving. Note: Drain off any excess yogurt juice or cucumber juices just before serving.

OTHER CONDIMENTS

Chopped peanuts, mango chutney or sweet India relish and sambal oelek (hot chili pepper condiment, available in the specialty sections of food stores; it's hot so use sparingly).

NASI GORENG SIDE DISHES

SHRIMP INDONESIAN

INGREDIENTS
¼ cup butter
2 lb medium raw shrimp, peeled and rinsed
2 medium onions, chopped coarsely
4 celery stalks, sliced ¼-inch on the diagonal
½ to 1 tsp sambal oelek, or to taste
2 tbsp peeled fresh ginger, finely chopped
Salt and pepper to taste
1 tbsp cornstarch
¼ cup warm water
1 cup chicken stock
1 cup canned coconut milk

DIANE'S SECRETS

Doug and I don't like our food too spicy, but if you really want to spice it up a notch or two, go for it!

METHOD

Melt the butter in a fry pan. Add the shrimp and sauté until opaque. Add onions, celery, sambal oelek, ginger, salt and pepper. Sauté a few minutes.

Blend the cornstarch and water and add mixture to chicken stock and coconut milk, mixing well. Pour stock mixture into sauté pan and stir until slightly thickened. May be refrigerated and reheated just before serving.

CHICKEN SATÉS

INGREDIENTS

¾ tsp ground ginger
2½ tsp ground coriander
Pinch each salt and pepper
5 tbsp lime juice
½ cup peanut or vegetable oil
2 large, whole chicken breasts, skinned and
    boned, cut into 1-inch pieces
½ cup toasted coconut (see Toasted
    Coconut, page 97)

METHOD

Soak 12 wooden skewers in water for about 3 hours. In a bowl, combine ginger, coriander, salt, pepper, lime juice and oil. Toss the chicken cubes in the marinade and refrigerate for several hours

Pre-heat the broiler or barbecue. Thread the chicken pieces on the wooden skewers. Brush the chicken with the marinade and barbecue or broil, turning once until done, about 8 to 10 minutes. Coat with the toasted coconut and arrange on serving platters.

BROILED BANANAS

INGREDIENTS
5 firm, barely ripe bananas
⅓ cup butter, melted
3 tbsp brown sugar
½ tsp cinnamon

METHOD

For the broiler: Peel the bananas, slice in half lengthwise and cut each half crosswise into 3-inch pieces. Arrange in a shallow baking dish. Combine the melted butter with the sugar and cinnamon. Drizzle evenly over the bananas. (May be covered and set aside at room temperature until ready to serve.)

Just before serving, broil until lightly browned.

For the barbecue: Lay the bananas on top of heavy-duty aluminum foil and drizzle the melted butter mixture over top. Seal well. Place on barbecue about 10 minutes before serving, turning once.

MUSHROOMS WITH PEPPERS

INGREDIENTS
2 tbsp butter
½ tsp ground cumin, to taste
Pinch red pepper flakes
1 lb mushrooms, cut into thick slices
2 red peppers, cut in julienne strips
1 yellow pepper, cut in julienne strips
Salt and pepper

METHOD

Melt the butter in a fry pan. Stir in cumin and red pepper flakes. Add the vegetables and sauté until just tender. Don't overcook. Add salt and pepper to taste. (May be prepared ahead and reheated before serving.)

IRISH SODA BREAD

MAKES 1 LOAF

There's nothing more pleasurable then the aroma of bread baking in the oven, then biting into the warm, fresh homemade loaf! For those who fear baking anything with yeast, this bread is for you! It's been my standby for over 30 years. It never fails and is great with hearty soups and stews.

INGREDIENTS
2 cups whole wheat flour
2 cups all-purpose flour
2 tsp double acting baking powder
1 tsp salt
1 tsp baking soda
2 tbsp brown sugar
1 large egg, beaten
2 cups buttermilk
Large oatmeal flakes

METHOD
Combine flours, baking powder, salt, baking soda, and brown sugar in a large bowl. Mix the egg with the buttermilk and stir into the dry ingredients just to blend. Dust the counter with oatmeal flakes. Turn out dough and knead about 10 times to cover with flakes and form a round ball. Cut a cross lightly on top of the loaf, place on buttered cookie sheet and bake at 375°F for 45 to 50 minutes or until it sounds hollow when tapped on the bottom.

PREPARATION TIME: 15 minutes

DIANE'S SECRETS

For a breakfast treat, add 1 cup dried fruit (raisins, chopped apricots, etc.) and 1 tsp cinnamon to the dry ingredients. Always serve warmed or toasted. This loaf can be made several hours before serving and reheated by wrapping in aluminum foil and placing in a 350°F oven for 10 minutes. It also freezes well. To serve, thaw overnight and reheat.

I had the pleasure of meeting Julia Child when our Westcoast Culinary Society hosted the International Association of Culinary Professionals' conference in Vancouver. She was our honourary chairperson. For her sold-out cooking demonstration she announced that she would do breads, which stunned everyone. Former food editor for the Vancouver Sun, Barbara McQuade, turned to me and exclaimed, "Why would she choose to do breads? It's so boring watching yeast rise!" But 10 minutes into starting her bread batters, we realized that Julia's dramatic flair made breadmaking look like a Broadway performance. She was swinging five to six different dough batters into the air, and continued to knead the remaining batters with the finesse of a plastic surgeon. In the middle of all this she lost her voice, which made her presentation a real challenge. Fortunately, her assistant stepped in to help explain the techniques. Everyone in the room was excited with the numerous varieties of breads that were made and passed around for us to sample. Copies of her recipes, with all the secrets for making a perfect loaf of bread were quickly snapped up. It was a triumphant afternoon. &

"HELLO DOLLY" SQUARES

If the fifties and sixties were the decades of lemon tarts and warmed brownie pudding desserts, the seventies was definitely the decade of "squares." There are many versions of this square; this is just one of them. I don't know if the original name for these squares was different, but these were probably named in honour of Carol Channing's debut in her highly successful Broadway opening of the musical *Hello Dolly*. I dedicate this recipe to my "three divas": Devine Elden, Helen Nachtigal and Jeto Hundal, who would be stars on any stage! They have been my assistants for over 25 years for my television presentations, film festival and sport receptions and all my book launches. They are true friends.

INGREDIENTS
⅓ cup melted butter
1½ cup packed crushed vanilla or graham wafers
1 package (6 oz) semi-sweet chocolate chips
1 cup flaked coconut
1 cup pecans or walnuts, finely chopped
1 can (14 oz) sweetened condensed milk

METHOD
Pour the melted butter evenly in a 9x13-inch baking pan. Sprinkle the wafers evenly over top. Pat down gently. Over the wafer base, sprinkle evenly the remaining ingredients in order: chocolate chips, coconut, nuts and sweetened condensed milk. Bake 25 minutes at 350°F or until golden and firm on top. Cool and cut into squares. Store in covered container.

PREPARATION TIME: 15 minutes

DIANE'S SECRETS

For an "over the top" square: Melt in a small saucepan 1 package (6 oz) semi-sweet chocolate chips with ½ cup creamy peanut butter, mixing until creamy and smooth. Spread evenly over the squares. Cool about 30 minutes. Chill in refrigerator before cutting.

EMERALD ISLE MALLOW

A fitting finale to a St. Paddy's day dinner party. Crème de menthe, which was the liqueur of the day in the seventies, makes an appearance in this after-dinner treat. A little goes a long way!

INGREDIENTS
1 lb marshmallows
¼ cup whole milk
6 tbsp green crème de menthe liqueur
3 cups whipping cream, divided
12 ladyfingers (approx.)
Chocolate curls

METHOD
Melt the marshmallows in the milk in a heavy saucepan on low heat, stirring constantly until smooth. Remove from heat and stir in the crème de menthe. Cool. Whip 2 cups of the whipping cream until stiff. Fold into the cooled marshmallow mixture.

Line bottom and sides of a 10-inch springform pan with ladyfingers. Carefully pour the marshmallow mixture over top. Chill 8 to 12 hours.

To serve, whip the remaining 1 cup cream until stiff. Remove from springform pan and place on a serving platter. Spoon whipped cream on top and decorate with chocolate curls.

PREPARATION TIME: 10 minutes

MOCHA PAVLOVA

In 1974 Doug and I visited New Zealand to attend the Commonwealth Games in Auckland. After the Games, we attended the World Congress in Sports Medicine in Melbourne, Australia before returning home. It had been 18 years since we had competed in the Olympic Games in Melbourne, so it was a special occasion to visit all the sights we had enjoyed in 1956. In both New Zealand and Australia, we enjoyed the traditional pavlova dessert. There's quite a rivalry between the two countries, each one claiming to be the original creator of this dessert. On that trip we were treated to this chocolate version. It's best made on the day of serving, although it could sit overnight in the refrigerator.

INGREDIENTS
4 large egg whites
Pinch cream of tartar
Pinch salt
1 cup berry sugar, extra fine granulated
1 tsp white vinegar
1 tsp instant coffee powder
2 tsp Dutch cocoa powder
1 tbsp cornstarch

FILLING
1 tsp instant coffee powder
2 tbsp Kahlúa
1 cup whipping cream
1 tbsp icing sugar
1 tbsp cocoa (optional)
Shaved chocolate

METHOD

In a medium-size bowl, beat the egg whites, cream of tartar and salt until stiff. Gradually add the sugar a spoonful at a time, beating after each addition until thoroughly blended. Fold in vinegar, coffee powder and cornstarch. Line a cookie sheet with aluminum foil or parchment paper and mound the stiff mixture into a 9-inch circle. Bake for 1 to 1½ hours, at 275°F until the outside is firm. Turn off oven; leave in oven with door closed to cool. It will crack slightly and sink a little in the middle.

Just before serving, prepare the filling. Dissolve the coffee powder in the Kahlúa and combine with the whipping cream and icing sugar in a bowl. Beat just until thickened. (Don't overbeat or it will turn into butter.) Add cocoa. Fill the meringue with the mixture. Decorate with shaved chocolate.

PREPARATION TIME: 1½ to 2 hours including baking time

DIANE'S SECRETS

Use fresh eggs at room temperature before beating. Be sure to beat each spoonful of sugar into the eggs thoroughly before adding the next spoonful.
This technique is important for the pavlova's success. Aluminum foil works particularly well on your baking tray. Cover the tray with one layer; do not grease. Place the pavlova mixture directly on the foil.
Bake, and when cool, peel off the foil gently.
Keep the pavlova in an airtight tin in the refrigerator. Sliced fresh strawberries, mango and kiwi fruit make excellent accompaniments to this wonderful dessert.

STRAWBERRIES MELBA

The story goes that revered chef Georges Auguste d'Escoffier created a special peach dessert for a famous opera star, Nellie Melba, when she was appearing in London and staying at the hotel where he worked. She loved it so much that he named it Peach Melba. The next morning she requested something light for breakfast. D'Escoffier, having just prepared some dry toast for the hotel guests, sent some along on her breakfast tray, calling it Melba Toast. This strawberry version of d'Escoffier's dessert adds a little twist to the original recipe.

INGREDIENTS
2 quarts fresh strawberries, washed, patted dry and hulled
3 tbsp icing sugar
1 package (10 oz) frozen raspberries in syrup, thawed
2 tbsp kirsch or orange liqueur
1 tsp fresh lemon juice
8 meringue shells, from bakery
Vanilla ice cream
Fresh mint sprigs

METHOD

If strawberries are large, slice them in half. Place in bowl with icing sugar and toss to coat. Set aside at room temperature.

In a food processor, purée raspberries with syrup. Strain, and add the liqueur and lemon juice.

Place meringue shells in champagne or sherbet dishes. Put a good-size scoop of ice cream in each shell. Top with sliced strawberries and raspberry purée. Decorate with mint.

PREPARATION TIME: 10 minutes

DIANE'S SECRETS

The raspberry purée can be made a day or two ahead and refrigerated. Strawberries can be prepared a few hours before serving.

Georges Auguste d'Escoffier was known as "the great king of cooks, and the cook of kings." Both amateur and professional chefs throughout this century have revered his books. He is the master of all master French chefs, and there is a museum in his memory in the village of Loubet in Provence, where he was born. I was thrilled and excited to visit his museum during our summer in Provence in 1999.

There are many Auguste d'Escoffier affiliations worldwide, including Les Dames d'Escoffier International. In 1997, as President of the Vancouver chapter, I had the privilege of hosting our Les Dames d'Escoffier dinner at the Sutton Place Hotel in Vancouver, honouring the great chef's 150th anniversary worldwide.

One of the current disciples of d'Escoffier is Jacques Pépin. His how-to cookbooks La Methode and La Technique set worldwide record sales in the seventies. Jacques has worked closely with Julia Child throughout the decades. In 1998 he joined his daughter Claudine on a new television series, as well as teaming up with Julia in 1999 in another televison series starring the two culinary greats. He continues to write best-selling cookbooks and travel the world sharing his incredible culinary expertise, just as the master chef d'Escoffier did in his era.

I had the opportunity to learn from Jacques at one of his classes held at Bonnie Stern's superb cooking school in Toronto. Bonnie had raced all over Toronto to find the perfect truffle for him, and finally purchased one from a top restaurant for $80. When Jacques was ready to add it to his dish, he smelled it, sliced it, then exclaimed: "Not good enough. Can't use it!" Jacques Pépin is the gold medal chef and his ingredients must be perfect. So truffles we did not taste that day! ✍

GLENYS MORGAN'S GÂTEAU AU CHOCOLAT

There are many variations of this French classic made famous by Julia Child. Glenys Morgan was our head chef at the Tomato when we first opened, and her version had customers in ecstasy. One of our customers exclaimed, "This cake is almost better than sex!" Glenys is now one of the most successful and sought after cooking school instructors in British Columbia, and her cake is the ultimate!

INGREDIENTS
¼ cup currants, just covered with Scotch to soak
8 oz semi-sweet chocolate (Lindt or Callebaut brands)
5 tbsp espresso coffee or Kahlúa liqueur
½ cup soft butter
3 large eggs, separated
⅔ cup white sugar
¼ cup all-purpose flour
⅔ cup finely ground almonds

METHOD
Soak the currants in Scotch. Meanwhile, butter well and flour a round 9-inch cake pan and line the bottom with parchment paper. Melt the chocolate completely with the espresso, then stir in the butter in small amounts. Set aside. Beat together the egg yolks and sugar until creamy, about 5 minutes. Add the cooled chocolate, Scotch and currants, flour and almonds.

Beat the egg whites until firm. Fold a few spoonfuls of the egg whites into the chocolate batter, then gently fold the rest of the whites in. Bake at 375°F for 25 minutes or until a skewer inserted in the centre comes out clean. Don't overbake.

When cool, remove from pan and put on a serving plate. Ice the entire cake with Ganache (below). Serve with fresh berries.

GANACHE

In a small saucepan, melt 1 cup semi-sweet Lindt or Callebaut chocolate, cut into chunks, in 1 cup whipping cream, stirring constantly until smooth and creamy. Cool slightly, and glaze the entire cake. Refrigerate until about 1 hour before serving.

PREPARATION TIME: 15 minutes

DIANE'S SECRETS

*This cake can be served without the Ganache,
but it is so wonderful and decadent with it!
This chocolate centrepiece is a chocolate copy of the
works of a world-renowned French painter, Vasarely.*

The seventies was definitely Julia Child's decade. She made culinary history with her new television cooking show Julia Child and Company, along with her companion cookbooks. Through television, she came into our homes and simplified classic French cooking for the amateur cook. Even today, in her late eighties, Julia Child is still the prima donna of the culinary world. There is no "heiress apparent"; there is and will always be only one Julia.

Her wise philosophy on eating is "everything in moderation." Her rich dishes are not for everyday indulgence, but when you feel the urge once and a while to treat yourself, don't feel guilty. Just don't go overboard, and take a pleasurable walk the next morning!

Now that's moderation! 🚲

The Exuberant

The Exuberant Eighties

WHILE THE SEVENTIES WERE YEARS THAT TEASED OUR PALATES FOR MORE — MORE HOME entertaining, more large cocktail parties and more dinner parties – by the end of the decade most of us had begun searching for a more balanced lifestyle. As we ushered in the eighties, the rum punches, rich French desserts and decadent parties gave way to a healthier approach in recipes such as Gin-Gingered Prawns (page 120), Campbell River Grilled Salmon (page 150) and Charmaine's Fast and Spicy Roveretto Spaghetti (page 144). Those years marked the debut of organic produce and "less fat, less sugar, less salt" were the buzzwords.

Fannie Merritt Farmer, renowned food writer in the early 1900s, was well ahead of her time when she predicted the trend toward a healthy diet in her 1924 cookbook: "I certainly feel that the time is not too far distant when a knowledge of the principles of diet will be an essential part of one's education. Then mankind will eat to live, will be able to do better mental and physical work, and disease will be less frequent." It took six decades from the time of Fannie Merritt Farmer's wise words for our society to begin to recognize the importance of making changes to our lifestyle through improved diet and more exercise.

My own appreciation for the need for change developed close to home. In the late seventies, Doug developed an irregular heart condition, or arrhythmia, known as paroxysmal auricular fibrillation. For two former Olympians who ran marathons and maintained a relatively good balance of diet and exercise, this was a significant wake-up call! And knowing that my cookbooks, *Chef on the Run,* published in 1982, and *More Chef on the Run,* published in 1984, included some very high-fat recipes, I had to address this issue.

Quick breads were ever-so-popular in the eighties – no need to fuss with yeast and wait for the bread to rise. Quick breads did the job, freezing beautifully and ready for serving in any emergency – or at any time. Even today I like to have one or two loaves in my freezer.

I remember so clearly one afternoon, as I was loading my boxes with ingredients to do a cooking session at a kitchen boutique, Doug peering over the food and exclaiming, "Who are we killing tonight, Diane?" I had lots of butter, cream cheese, sour cream, mayonnaise and liqueur packed alongside the fresh ingredients. On the way to my cooking class, all I could think of was Doug's comment.

As it turned out, I was leaving in two days for my cross-Canada book tour for *More Chef on the Run.* But I was devastated by Doug's comment and when I returned home from the class, I declared to him, "I can't do this tour, telling everyone to make rich dishes for their families, loaded with fat. What am I doing?" Doug eased my distress with his wisdom, reminding me that I also had many healthy dishes and that what was needed was balance, a healthy diet combined with a healthy dose of exercise.

I left for my book tour, feeling better, but on my return I said to Doug, "We are going to write a lifestyle book together." *Chef and Doctor on the Run,* published in 1986, became my most challenging book, but also the most rewarding. It proved to me that recipes with less sugar, less salt and less fat can still taste sensational, as Black Bean Soup (page 132), Marcelle's Low-Fat Tuscan Cheesecake (page 156) and Oriental Noodle Salad (page 128), all featured in this chapter, demonstrate.

In 1988 I began working on *Fresh Chef on the Run,* which was to be launched in the fall of 1990. I thought it would be my last book. I could never have imagined, at that time, that in 1991 my daughter Jennifer, Haik Gharibians, Jamie Norris and I would open our restaurant, The Tomato Fresh Food Café, and follow up with a book on the café in 1995! Both books emphasized the lower-fat, healthier recipes that we had embraced.

The renewed interest in food, dining and entertaining was reflected in thriving cookbook sales. Martha Stewart made her big debut on the culinary scene in 1982 with her sophisticated cookbook *Entertaining,* and her signature huge baskets filled with strawberries. Julia Child and Jacques Pépin just kept producing fabulous cookbooks, and California spa cookbooks were popular with their lighter approach to dining. The hot cooking magazines continued to be *Gourmet, Bon Appetit* and *Food and Wine.* The superb Australian *Vogue Entertaining* also entered the scene.

Chefs were treated like Hollywood celebrities, as patrons flocked to their restaurants to enjoy their signature dishes and just to be "seen." Two high-profile chefs of the time were California's Wolfgang Puck, chef to the stars with his gourmet pizzas and chic Los Angeles restaurant Spago, and Alice Waters, who started the trend toward local produce and regional cuisine from her Chez Panisse restaurant in Berkeley, starring her wild greens with chèvre. There were also Canadian chefs I admired and learned from in the eighties and who are still going strong, including Toronto chef and cookbook author Jamie Kennedy and Bonnie Stern with her best-selling cookbooks, television series and cooking school. In Vancouver, Umberto Menghi began his highly successful restaurant empire. Nicky Major, Susan Newson, Susan Mendelson, Leslie Stowe and Linda Meinhardt were thriving with their catering and deli establishments. It was a great decade for entertaining, and I was inspired by all of these talented chefs.

The importance of adding more fresh vegetables and hearty grains to our diets was very much evident in the eighties. Chefs were big on pilafs, featuring barley, bulgur wheat and five- or six-grain rices. Arborio rice was commonplace and "risotto parties" were popular. Puréed vegetables were a simple and elegant addition to any plate, and "gratins" were making a comeback, but without the heavy cream and cheeses. Gutsy ethnic bean dishes with lentil, fava, black, turtle or kidney beans were added to restaurant menus.

Vegetables never looked and tasted so good! ॐ

During this time, Doug and I found many reasons to be travelling around the world. In 1981, I was appointed one of two general managers for the Canadian Olympic athletic team. In that role, my responsibilities were mainly media liaison and protocol for our team. Doug and I were also becoming increasingly involved in presenting lifestyle seminars around the world, and we attended many international sports medicine symposiums. In total, we visited 17 different countries during the eighties. Our travels gave me the opportunity to enjoy dining in restaurants, meeting chefs and learning more about different cuisines. Whenever the opportunity arose and they were out of school, Jennifer and Rand accompanied us on our travels.

My decision to be guest chef at the popular new cooking kitchens opening up in various kitchen boutiques added to my hectic schedule. Although it was more work to load my car full of ingredients and serving dishes rather than hosting the classes in my own kitchen as I had done in the seventies, it was fun teaching in different settings. I taught at many of Vancouver's kitchen boutiques as well as in Kelowna, Kamloops, Victoria, Calgary and other cities, launching my latest menus. I was definitely "on the run"! It was great to be able to get feedback on which recipes were the most successful, and most important, which recipes students would recreate in their own kitchens.

In looking back at the eighties, I think they were the most challenging and exciting of my culinary career. As busy as we were, we listened to the wake-up call that Doug's heart problem had given us. We consciously took the time to exercise, relax and enjoy our family and friends more. Our priority now is a balance of diet and exercise. There is no guarantee that a healthier balance will add years to our lives, but with any luck it will add life to our years!

So with these thoughts, and in celebration of the exuberant eighties, I am excited to share with you my gold medal recipes of that decade. Enjoy the jump-start drink of the day, The Fitness Group Smoothie (page 115), The BC Hot House Sunpower Moroccan Salad for lunch on the go (page 126), Chef Michael Noble's Wild Rice Risotto with Parmesan Cups for a taste of Italy at dinner (page 140), and end your day with a melt-in-your-mouth Hot Apricot Soufflé with Mango Purée (page 158). Who said healthy eating had to be dull and tasteless?

One of the hardest challenges for me when I was working on Chef and Doctor on the Run *back in the eighties was coming up with low-fat desserts that actually tasted like dessert. These recipes are the winners from the dozens I experimented with. I believe that once in a while, for a special treat, you can indulge in your favourite rich dessert. Just remember, beautiful things come in small packages! In other words, enjoy after-dinner indulgences in moderation. Years ago, I might have eaten a half pint of my favourite ice cream; now a small scoop will satisfy my craving!* ॐ

THE FITNESS GROUP SMOOTHIE

I call this my drink my jump start for the day. It was originally featured at the juice bar of the Fitness Group, the fitness centre where I've been working out ever since it opened in Vancouver in the eighties. The owner, Barbara Crompton, and Julie McNeney, communications director, featured this smoothie as an après-workout drink. At the Tomato Café, we've been serving it ever since we opened, and it's as popular as ever. I also demonstrate this smoothie drink at the lifestyle seminars that I do with Doug. Use your own creative talents and add other flavoured yogurts and fruit!

INGREDIENTS
½ cup skim milk
½ cup French vanilla or fruit-based yogurt
1 tbsp wheat germ
1 ripe banana, sliced in large chunks
1 cup fresh or frozen strawberries
5 ice cubes (only if fruit is fresh)

METHOD
Put all ingredients in a blender and blend at high speed for a few seconds.

PREPARATION TIME: 5 minutes

SUSI Q

Topping the charts at the Tomato Café is the Susi Q, named in honour
our daughter-in-law Suzanne. Strawberries, oranges and bananas are
the winning trio!

INGREDIENTS
1 ripe banana
5 strawberries, fresh or frozen
2 cups fresh squeezed orange juice

METHOD
Put all ingredients in a blender and blend at high speed for a
few seconds.

PREPARATION TIME: 5 minutes

New York's Algonquin Hotel had its famous Round Table. Vancouver's Tomato Fresh Food
Café has its Tomato Club, and I don't mean a sandwich! Wednesday lunchtime
diners may have seen Tomato enthusiasts Wendy Kendal and me, founders of the venture,
sporting our brightly coloured Tomato Club badges. Formed in 1998, the club commemorates
my wife, Sharon Waddell, a long-time Tomato fan, whose untimely death in an automobile
accident had occurred earlier that year.

As a gourmet and architect who lives and works in the neighbourhood, I was
instrumental in the 1996 expansion of the then-tiny restaurant which was bursting at its
seams. Fellow tomato lover Wendy Kendal just likes good food. She is a local family
physician who extols the virtues of a healthy diet to her patients. Everyone wants a food
experience like Tomato just around the corner. I'm lucky to have the original!

BY BERNARD MOTTET

CHUTNEY CHEESE TORTE

SERVES 25 TO 30

This cheese appetizer with a hint of curry has been my lifesaver for many functions over the past 20 years. From sports medicine symposiums for over 250 participants, to athletic events and film festival receptions, to festive family occasions, I've made hundreds of these tortes. This recipe is on our catering menu at the Tomato Café and has appeared at many Vancouver theatre opening-night galas! It can be made a day or two ahead of time.

Less fat: Use low-fat cheeses and low-fat sour cream.

INGREDIENTS
12 oz Philadelphia solid cream cheese
2 cups grated Monterey Jack cheese
2 cups grated sharp Cheddar cheese
¼ tsp Dijon mustard
Dash Worcestershire sauce
1 large clove garlic, crushed
1 tsp mild Madras curry powder
1 tbsp mayonnaise
1 tbsp sour cream
⅓ cup green onions, finely chopped

TOPPING
½ cup chutney, finely chopped
½ cup green onions, finely chopped
½ red pepper, thinly sliced in julienne strips

METHOD
In a large food processor or electric mixer, combine all ingredients except those for the topping. If your food processor is small, process the mix in two batches. Blend until smooth and creamy.

Line the bottom of a 9- or 10-inch springform pan with parchment or wax paper. Evenly spread the cheese mixture on the bottom of the pan; cover and chill. Just before serving, remove the torte from the pan, turning upside down on a serving platter; remove the paper. Spread an even thin layer of the chutney over the torte. Decorate the outside ring with the chopped green onions and a few slices of red pepper. Provide one or two cheese knives on the platter.

Serve with plenty of Carr's Water Biscuits or other plain crackers.

DIANE'S SECRETS

It's important to use a solid cream cheese, not the soft, spreadable type. For the chutney, Major Grey's or other fruit-style chutneys work well.

PREPARATION TIME: 20 minutes

HAIK'S HAPPY STICKS

MAKES ABOUT 4 DOZEN

This recipe was given to me by Haik Gharibians in the early eighties, and it has become a family tradition for many of our parties. I always think of Haik whenever I roll up these finger-length morsels, which were his signature appetizer. Make them ahead, freeze them, pop them in the oven, stack them on a tray, then watch them disappear! They are a super "emergency appetizer."

INGREDIENTS
14 oz feta cheese
3 large eggs, slightly beaten
3 tbsp fresh dill, finely chopped
1 lb phyllo pastry
1½ cups butter

METHOD
A few hours before assembling, crumble the feta cheese well. Add the eggs and dill. Refrigerate several hours to thicken slightly.

Heat the butter in a small saucepan until lukewarm. Pat your hands with a little of the butter, then using your hands, lightly brush one sheet of phyllo on both sides. Cut the sheet into three equal lengthwise strips. Fold each strip into thirds to form a square. Spread a good teaspoon of the cheese mixture along one edge, and roll up very tightly jelly roll fashion to form a stick or finger. Repeat with all the phyllo and filling. Place sticks as you go in a plastic container in layers, with parchment or wax paper in between. Seal well and freeze until ready to serve.

To serve, place sticks well apart on an ungreased cookie sheet and bake at 375°F for 8 to 10 minutes or until crisp and golden.

Serve immediately.

PREPARATION TIME: 1 hour

DIANE'S SECRETS

The phyllo pastry must be rolled very tightly to prevent it from coming apart when baking. The unbaked sticks will keep for up to 3 to 4 months in the freezer if stored in a plastic container and sealed well.

Haik Gharibians was both a friend and a partner, along with my daughter Jennifer and Jamie Norris, when we first opened our Tomato Café in 1991. Haik entertained with flare and elegance.

He passed away in 1997, and Jennifer and I sadly miss him for his wisdom, patience and friendship. Haik travelled the world as the physiotherapist for the Canadian national swim team and the American figure skating team to many Olympics and world championships. We loved exchanging the latest international gossip of the sports we were involved in, as well as the latest recipes we brought home from our trips.

Whenever Haik travelled, he would return with a unique dish or bowl for entertaining, and it had to be HUGE! After one trip to Europe, he arrived with what had to be the largest fry pan in the world, at least 5 feet wide and 10 inches deep. We used this pan, which ran on propane, for many parties to cook quesadillas, salmon, chops and other foods. It always caused a sensation, making it well worth the challenging task of lifting it out of Haik's van!

PITA TRIANGLES

MAKES 48 TRIANGLES

These crisp crackers made from pita bread are great with dips, spreads, soups and salads – or just to munch on, instead of potato chips! Try them with Eileen's Olive Tapenade (page 177) or Sun-Dried Tomato Chèvre (page 135).

INGREDIENTS
4 white or whole wheat pita rounds
Light olive or vegetable oil

METHOD
Cut the pita bread across horizontally to make two thin rounds out of each. Brush a little of the oil on one side of each round, and cut each half into 6 triangles. Bake on a cookie sheet at 300°F for 10 to 12 minutes or until golden.

Can be cooled and stored for several days in an airtight container. Reheat in a 300°F oven for a few minutes to crisp, if needed.

PREPARATION TIME: 10 minutes

GIN-GINGERED PRAWNS

In 1985, Doug and I attended the World Cup of Athletics in Canberra, Australia. We stayed at one of the local hotels, which boasted one of the top chefs in Australia. One evening, he served Gin-Gingered Prawns as the feature appetizer. They were so good that I ate three orders for my evening meal! I complimented him and ordered them every evening until we left.

The combination of gin, Japanese pickled ginger and green onions is the perfect teaser for the delicate flavour of the prawns. I have made this "down under" appetizer for parties, cooking demonstrations, fundraisers and whenever we've had a craving for them! We have also featured it on our menu at the Tomato Café.

In 1985, Doug and I were coach and manager, respectively, of the first ever World Cup of Marathons for men and women, held in Hiroshima, Japan. We enjoy Japanese food, so it was a special treat to be invited to a reception honouring the participating teams from around the world. The invitation stated that it was from 7:00 p.m. to 9:00 p.m., and our team arrived at the immense ballroom at 7:00 p.m. precisely! It was a Japanese feast with giant sake barrels being cracked open by very strong sumo wrestlers, dancers and musicians performing, and Japanese chefs preparing their specialty dishes at several food stations. It was a spectacular evening. The teams were enjoying the ▶

INGREDIENTS
4 to 5 tbsp butter
2/3 cup green onions, finely chopped
36 medium-sized raw prawns, thawed and peeled
3 tbsp pickled Japanese ginger, well drained
   and chopped
1/4 cup gin
1 baguette, thinly sliced and warmed

METHOD

Melt the butter in a large fry pan. Add the onions and sauté briefly. Add the prawns and sauté 2 minutes more. Add the ginger and gin and continue to cook for a minute or two longer, just until the prawns are opaque. Do not overcook or they will be tough. Put into a serving dish, drizzle with sauce from the pan and serve. Pass the warmed bread for dipping into the sauce.

PREPARATION TIME: 5 minutes

DIANE'S SECRETS

Pickled ginger can be found at most specialty Asian or fish markets. This dish is not the same using fresh ginger; the marriage of pickled ginger and gin is the key (and it doesn't have to be expensive gin!).
For more people, if you increase the number of prawns, you must also increase the amount of sauce to have plenty for dipping. If you prefer, you can serve these prawns in individual scallop shells as a first course.

opportunity to relax after having run the grueling marathon, and they were in no hurry to leave. But when 9:00 p.m. arrived, the sake barrels were quickly removed, entertainment abruptly ended and the chefs all disappeared. We soon realized that our Japanese organizers were as efficient in hosting the reception as they were in hosting the World Cup marathon! Protocol is strictly adhered to in Japan, and everyone respects the time frame stated on invitations. This is so different from North America, where we tend to let the party go on until the last guests leave. It may have been the shortest reception our Canadian team has ever attended, but it was one of the most memorable!

TOMATO, PEPPER, ONION RELISH
(PEPERONATA)

One of our most memorable travel experiences was in 1989 when Doug and I took off for Turkey. We had no obligations, no teams to worry about, no meetings to attend. It was solely a vacation to explore and discover Turkey by bus and to enjoy the fabulous ethnic cuisine. One of our most distinct memories of Turkish food was the aroma of freshly baked bread coming from the bakeries early in the morning as we prepared to board the bus for the next village. We would rush in to pick up a loaf before our departure, and often the owners would sell a tasty relish as a spread.

Heather Vogt, a talented former chef at our Tomato Café, used a similar relish combination in our special Mediterranean Grilled sandwich. Whenever I had the sandwich, it would bring back memories of our trip to Turkey. Here is the version that I developed for BC Hot House. It's a super spread for baguettes and crackers, to add to your favourite sandwich or to serve tossed with pasta. It also freezes well, most conveniently in 1-cup containers.

INGREDIENTS
Olive oil
1 cup red onions, coarsely chopped
3 sweet peppers, 1 each of red, yellow and orange, coarsely chopped
4 large cloves garlic, peeled
5 large tomatoes, cored, sliced in half and seeded
2 tbsp olive oil
½ cup pimento-stuffed olives, or a combination of green and black olives, chopped coarsely
Pinch red pepper flakes
½ tsp cumin, or to taste
1 tsp sweet Spanish or Hungarian paprika
1 tsp sugar
2 tbsp sherry vinegar or white wine vinegar
¼ cup parsley, chopped

METHOD

Heat the oven to 400°F. Coat 2 large cookie sheets with olive oil.

In a bowl, toss the onions, peppers and garlic with a little olive oil to coat. Spread in one layer on a cookie sheet and roast for 15 minutes. Remove garlic, chop coarsely, and return it to the vegetables. Toss together and roast 10 to 15 minutes more until softened. Set aside.

In a bowl, toss the tomatoes with a little olive oil. Place the tomato halves, cut side up, on the second cookie sheet. Roast for 15 minutes. Turn cut side down, and roast another 10 to 15 minutes. Lift the skins from each tomato half and discard. Chop tomatoes coarsely, blending in any juices from the cookie sheet. Set aside

In a large fry pan, heat the 2 tbsp olive oil. Add the onions, peppers, garlic and tomatoes. Stir to blend well. Add the rest of the ingredients and simmer uncovered on low heat for 10 to 15 minutes or until thickened to a spreading consistency. Cool.

Freeze or refrigerate. Will keep several days in the refrigerator.

PREPARATION TIME: 60 minutes

DIANE'S SECRETS *If you use black olives, look for Greek calamata or Spanish olives, or any black olives in salt brine.*

In 1984, the Olympic Games were held in Los Angeles. It was the first Olympic Games that made money by bringing in large sponsor corporations and selling exclusive television broadcast rights. It was a superior Games, and we were treated with the best food we've ever had at any international competition. The organizers brought in the top American and international chefs to create a global menu for all religious and dietary requirements. The dining rooms were open 24 hours a day, allowing all the participants to enjoy the wonderful choices of fresh produce, salads and high-carbohydrate foods that athletes love. We were totally spoiled! ☚

BAGEL CRISPS

Bagels were the all the rage in the eighties and bagel shops came up with every flavour imaginable. Bagels are at their best just out of the oven, so I like to use up my day-old bagels by making these crisps. Boasting only 21 calories per crisp, they are great as snackers or served with dips, spreads, soups and salads. As with Pita Triangles (page 119), these crisps are equally delicious with Eileen's Olive Tapenade (page 177) and Sun-dried Tomato Chèvre spread (page 135).

INGREDIENTS
4 whole wheat, plain, sesame or pumpernickel day-
  old bagels
Vegetable oil
3 to 4 cloves garlic, peeled and halved

METHOD
Slice the bagels in very thin horizontal slices. Brush both sides with a little oil, and place on one large or two medium cookie sheets. Spear half a garlic clove on a fork, cut side down, and rub both sides of bagel slices. As the clove loses its oil, replace it with another one.

Bake the bagel slices at 275°F for 50 minutes or until golden and crisp, turning them over at half time. Watch carefully that they don't get too dark. Cool on racks. Stored in a sealed container, these crisps will keep fresh for days.

PREPARATION TIME: 5 minutes

DIANE'S SECRETS *Cinnamon-raisin, apple and cheese bagels are all tasty choices for making these crisps. Omit the garlic if you use cinnamon-raisin or apple bagels.*

FRESH ASPARAGUS WITH GREEN PEPPERCORN DRESSING

SERVES 4

During the 1984 Olympic Games in Los Angeles, on a rare night off from the Olympic Village dining room, Doug and I had a chance to eat at Trumps, one of Los Angeles's top restaurants. This is my version of their unique and zesty dressing and salad. Try the dressing as well with a salad of prawns, melon and avocado slices on a bed of butter lettuce or Belgium endive in julienne strips!

INGREDIENTS

2 oz chèvre, cut into 2¼-inch round slices
½ tbsp vegetable oil
½ cup fresh bread crumbs made from whole wheat
  or French bread
24 spears fresh asparagus, peeled at stem, if desired
2 bunches argula or watercress
20 seedless green grapes, peeled

DRESSING

1 tbsp green peppercorns, washed and strained
1 cup green seedless grapes, skins on
3 tbsp vegetable oil

METHOD

DRESSING

Combine the peppercorns and grapes in the food processor and process until creamy. Slowly add the oil and blend until thickened. Refrigerate, covered, for up to several days. Shake well before using.

Dip the cheese slices in the vegetable oil; roll in bread crumbs to coat well. Refrigerate.

Trim and clean the asparagus and steam until cooked but still slightly crisp, about 2 minutes. Don't overcook. Cool quickly in a bowl of ice water, pat dry and refrigerate.

Just before serving, divide the asparagus among four plates lined with argula or watercress and drizzle a little of the dressing over each. Meanwhile, bake the cheese rounds at 400°F for 5 minutes. Cut each round in half and place a piece on top of the asparagus. Sprinkle each plate with peeled grapes. Pass more dressing at the table.

PREPARATION TIME: 20 minutes

Salads took front row centre in the eighties.

Menus featured salads often with eight or more exotic greens or with chèvre, bocconcini and Gorgonzola cheese. Warm salads were introduced and excited the palate. Here are my salad hits of the eighties – those that brought rave reviews and that continue to wow family and friends whenever I serve them.

DIANE'S SECRETS

You can find green peppercorns in specialty food sections of your market. They are packed in brine and have a unique fruity taste. Try them in sauces for meats and poultry for an interesting taste!

THE BC HOT HOUSE SUNPOWER
MOROCCAN SALAD

SERVES 10 TO 12

In 1984, Achilles International Track and Field Society, a non-profit society made up former track and field enthusiasts, with Doug as chairman, approached the *Vancouver Sun* newspaper with a proposal to sponsor a major 10-K fun run through the heart of Vancouver. The Sun management agreed, and we had 3,000 keen entries that first year. In 1999, we celebrated our 15th anniversary of the Vancouver Sun Run, with over 40,000 participating. It's now ranked among the top ten 10-K fun runs in the world.

In celebration of the 15th anniversary of the run, the *Sun*'s food section featured this recipe that I had developed for BC Hot House, one of the Sun Run's sponsors, as an ideal "fuel food" salad for the runners. It received rave reviews when I served it at our son Rand's running clinic, held at his sporting goods store, The Right Shoe.

It's a crunchy, colourful and nutritious salad that boasts the sensual spices of Morocco. Perfect for summer entertaining, barbecues, buffets, boating parties and picnics.

INGREDIENTS

4 cups small mushrooms, halved

4 cups small cherry tomatoes

1 can (19 oz) garbanzo beans or chick peas, drained

1 cup large black olives, halved, or whole calamata olives, pitted

2 cups celery, sliced on the diagonal

3 sweet peppers, 1 each of red, yellow and orange, thinly sliced

1 cup red onion, finely chopped

3 jalapeno peppers, seeded and finely chopped

⅓ cup fresh cilantro, chopped (optional)

Butter lettuce

1 English cucumber, sliced thinly on the diagonal and patted dry

DRESSING

¾ cup plain yogurt
1 cup mayonnaise
2 tbsp olive or vegetable oil
Juice of 1 large lemon or lime
2 large cloves garlic, crushed
Pepper to taste
2 to 3 tsp cumin, or to taste
2 to 3 tsp turmeric, or to taste
1 tsp mild Madras curry powder
¼ cup fresh dill, chopped

METHOD

DRESSING

Whisk together all dressing ingredients to blend. Refrigerate.

Several hours before serving, toss together all ingredients except lettuce and cucumber. Add the dressing and toss to coat the salad well. Cover and refrigerate.

To serve, spoon the salad on a bed of the butter lettuce, with cucumber slices arranged around the outside.

PREPARATION TIME: 30 minutes

DIANE'S SECRETS

For a "power lunch," try stuffing this salad in a pita bread pocket.

ORIENTAL NOODLE SALAD

In 1986, when Doug and I launched *Chef and Doctor on the Run*, we did a cross-Canada tour promoting our book. It was the first time that Doug joined me on the book promotion circuit, and it was a fun time for both of us. For many of our publicity events, we would demonstrate this salad and offer samples to our audience. It was interesting that many shopping malls appeared empty until the salad was complete and ready to serve. Dozens of people would then suddenly appear! It's best made a day ahead so the flavours can blend. The dressing is also great as a dip for prawns or grilled chicken.

INGREDIENTS

1 package (about ¾ lb) steam-fried or dry Chinese
    egg noodles for Chow Mein, or
    linguine
4 tsp pure sesame oil
¾ cup water chestnuts, finely chopped
½ cup green onions, chopped
½ cup red and yellow peppers, finely chopped
1 cup carrots, chopped and lightly blanched
    (1 to 2 minutes)
3 tbsp sesame seeds, toasted
    (see Diane's secrets, page 91)
½ cup unsalted cashew nuts, chopped

DRESSING

¼ cup smooth peanut butter
2 tbsp Chinese tamari sauce
2 tbsp soy sauce
2 cloves garlic, crushed
4 tsp pure sesame oil
2 tbsp rice wine vinegar or sherry
2 tbsp red pepper oil (see Diane's secrets, below)

METHOD

DRESSING

Blend all dressing ingredients in a food processor; refrigerate until ready to mix with the salad ingredients.

Boil noodles according to package directions; drain. Rinse well and toss with sesame oil. Mix well with the rest of the ingredients. Add the dressing and toss well. Cover and refrigerate overnight.

PREPARATION TIME: 40 minutes

DIANE'S SECRETS — *To make your own red pepper oil, add ½ tsp red pepper flakes to 2 tbsp oil. Bring to a boil and let sit for 5 minutes. Strain. Chinese specialty markets sell bottled red pepper oil, but you must use it with caution as it is often extremely hot! You may want to double the dressing recipe to have extra to add to the salad before serving or for passing at the table.*

FLAMING SPINACH SALAD

SERVES 6 TO 8

This spectacular flambéed salad offers a unique sweet and sour taste. A little reminder: be careful when lighting the dressing.

INGREDIENTS
3 bags (10-oz size) fresh spinach
1 lb bacon
2 oz brandy
3 hard boiled eggs
Sunflower seeds, toasted
(see Diane's secrets, page 91)

DRESSING
1/3 cup red wine vinegar
Juice of 1 lemon
1/4 cup granulated sugar
1/2 tsp Worcestershire sauce
1/4 to 1/2 tsp Dijon mustard, to taste

In 1982, I did a cross-Canada tour for my first book, Chef on the Run. I was particularly looking forward to appearing on Margaret Trudeau's television show in Ottawa, and I decided to present the most dramatic recipe in the book, which was Flaming Spinach Salad. Margaret was fantastic; she loves cooking, and she pitched right in to prepare the salad with me. Toward the end of the show, Margaret lit the Sterno in the chafing dish as I started to flame the brandy. All of a sudden, the paper towels at my feet were in flames! Some of the lit Sterno had dropped onto the towels and they had caught on fire. Thank heavens the floor director was on his final countdown to end the show! I quickly poured the hot dressing over the spinach, smiled at Margaret and we proceeded to taste the salad for the close of the show. At that moment, the whole studio was full of black pieces of burned paper towels. It was truly one of the most dramatic presentations I had ever done on television! Margaret and I had a great chuckle as we waved goodbye to the shocked camera crew. ॐ

METHOD

Remove stems from the spinach, wash and dry well and store in sealed plastic bags in the refrigerator until ready to serve (will keep fresh for two or three days). Fry the bacon until crisp; drain well, reserving the fat. Chop the bacon into small squares and refrigerate. Prepare dressing.

DRESSING

Whisk the first five dressing ingredients, then add the ¾ cup bacon fat and blend well. Refrigerate until ready to serve.

Just before serving, break the spinach leaves into bite-sized pieces and divide among 6 to 8 salad bowls. Mix the dressing in a skillet with the chopped bacon and heat until very hot. Pour into a chafing dish to bring to the table and keep hot over a candle. Heat the brandy in a small saucepan until it begins to vapourize, then pour it very slowly over the hot dressing and set it alight. Pour about 3 tbsp of the flaming dressing over each salad, and decorate with slices of egg and toasted sunflower seeds.

PREPARATION TIME: 25 minutes

Less fat: Substitute light olive or vegetable oil for the bacon fat and julienne of red peppers for the eggs. Limit the amount of dressing you use on the spinach.

BLACK TURTLE BEAN SOUP

SERVES 8 TO 10

You will be "full of beans," without a doubt, when you eat this hearty, healthy soup with only 595 calories per serving. It was one of the most requested recipes from my *Chef and Doctor on the Run* cookbook. It's a meal in itself, served with a selection of condiments.

INGREDIENTS
12 cups water
5 cups Mexican black beans, rinsed in cold water
4 cups chicken or vegetable stock
6 cloves garlic, finely chopped
1 bay leaf
1 red pepper, finely chopped
4 stalks celery, finely chopped
1 medium white onion, finely chopped
2 leeks, white part only, coarsely chopped
3 medium carrots, finely chopped
1½ tbsp ground cumin seed
1½ tbsp dried oregano
Salt and pepper to taste
Tabasco
½ cup Mexican salsa or mild taco sauce
⅓ cup sherry or dark rum (optional)

METHOD

Bring the water to boil in a large Dutch oven; add beans and boil for 5 minutes. Remove from heat and let beans steep, covered, for 90 minutes. Add the rest of the ingredients, except for the sherry; continue to simmer for 1 to 1½ hours, stirring frequently and skimming off the scum.

Remove the bay leaf. Add more stock if soup becomes too thick. Continue to cook for 1 more hour or until the beans are tender. Stir occasionally. Add sherry or rum.

Remove 3 cups of the soup and purée in a food processor or blender. Return puréed portion to remaining soup and stir well. Serve with an assortment of condiments such as Mexican salsa, chopped red and yellow peppers, chopped green onions, low-fat yogurt or sour cream, chopped cilantro or parsley, and lemon wedges.

PREPARATION TIME: 3 to 3½ hours, including cooking time

 DIANE'S SECRETS

Black or turtle beans can be found in most health-food stores. This soup is best made a day or two ahead of serving for the flavours to peak. It keeps up to three days in the refrigerator, and it also freezes well.

SWEET ONION SOUP, CALIFORNIA-STYLE

SERVES 4

This recipe is an adaptation of the talented Hawaiian chef Roy Yamaguchi's Maui onion soup. En route to New Zealand in 1985, we stopped off in Maui, where we first learned of Chef Yamaguchi. He has several restaurants and has written many cookbooks, and he's known for his sublime wine sauces and his Hawaiian regional cuisine. But it wasn't until 1999 that we dined at one of Chef Yamaguchi's famous Maui restaurants and enjoyed his innovative cuisine. Naturally, he uses the marvelously sweet Maui onions in his dishes, but any sweet onion works in this classic French soup served California-style with Sun-Dried Tomato Chèvre on crostinis.

INGREDIENTS

1 tbsp vegetable oil
3 sweet white onions, peeled, cut in half and sliced
    paper thin
2 large cloves garlic, crushed
6 cups chicken stock
Pinch each of salt and pepper, or to taste
8 thin slices (⅓-inch each) baguette
½ cup chèvre
6 softened sun-dried tomatoes, finely chopped
2 tbsp fresh basil, finely chopped
⅓ cup Parmesan cheese, freshly grated

METHOD

SOUP

(Can be made a day or two ahead of serving for the flavours to develop.) In a medium-size pot, heat the oil. Add the onions and garlic. Turn the heat to low and sauté until golden and softened, about 10 to 15 minutes. Stir frequently. Add the stock; simmer uncovered 30 to 40 minutes. Add the salt and pepper. Cool, then refrigerate.

SUN-DRIED TOMATO CHÈVRE

A day or two before serving: In a small bowl, blend together the chèvre, sun-dried tomatoes and basil. Refrigerate.

DAY OF SERVING

Heat the oven to 375°F. To prepare the crostinis, place the baguette slices on a cookie sheet and toast in oven 4 minutes per side, or until golden and crispy. Set aside. Just before serving, spread about 1 tbsp of the spread on each of the 8 crostinis. Sprinkle a little Parmesan cheese on top of each. Put on cookie sheet and bake at 375°F a few minutes to warm, while you simmer the soup.

To serve, ladle the soup into 4 small bowls. Top each with 2 crostinis.

PREPARATION TIME: 50 minutes

DIANE'S SECRETS

Sometimes I like to double the recipe for the chèvre spread, make extra crostinis and broil them to serve alongside the soup. The soup part of this recipe can be made in advance and refrigerated until ready to serve, but be sure to reheat thoroughly. My pet peeve is luke-warm soup; make sure it is boiling hot before serving, as it cools down quickly.

GAZPACHO

SERVES 8 TO 10

There are many variations of this Spanish chilled soup specialty. This version is chunky, not spicy, and is the one we've served at our Tomato Café since we opened. It's like a liquid salad, perfect for warding off hunger pangs between meals.

I use only red, orange or yellow peppers (as I do in all recipes that call for peppers) because many people cannot digest the green variety. Gazpacho keeps well in the refrigerator for about 4 days.

INGREDIENTS
4 very ripe large tomatoes
1 can (14 oz) tomatoes, including juice
½ onion
2 English cucumbers, unpeeled
2 red peppers, or 1 each of red, yellow or orange, seeded
4 sprigs parsley
2 cloves garlic, crushed
10 oz V-8 juice
2 cups tomato juice
Juice of ½ lemon
½ cup Heinz chili sauce (see Diane's secrets, below)
3 tbsp fresh basil, or ½ tsp dry
3 tbsp fresh dill, or ½ tsp dry
½ tsp sweet Spanish or Hungarian paprika
1 tbsp white wine vinegar
½ tsp Worcestershire sauce
Croutons (page 78)
Green onions, chopped

METHOD

At least 2 to 3 days before serving, cut the fresh and canned tomatoes, onion, cucumbers and peppers into chunks. Combine all in a food processor with the parsley, garlic, V-8 juice and tomato juice, processing a portion at a time with an on/off motion. Add the rest of the ingredients and blend slightly. Do not overprocess; the mixture should be chunky. (If you prefer a thinner soup, add more tomato juice and experiment with the herbs and seasonings until the soup is to your liking.) Cover and refrigerate.

Serve in small bowls and pass croutons and onions to sprinkle on top.

PREPARATION TIME: 30 minutes

 DIANE'S SECRETS *It is important to make this soup at least 2 days ahead of serving, allowing time for the flavours to peak. The key ingredient in my gazpacho is the Heinz chili sauce; it gives it that special punch. As well, using fresh herbs instead of dried makes a big difference in the freshness of the soup's taste.*

VEGETABLE GRATIN

SERVES 6

Here is my quick "emergency" vegetable dish that my family just loves. It's low in fat, high in taste, and it's your entire vegetable plate all in one dish. Make it ahead of time for a small or large crowd; it's easy to multiply! Add a roasted chicken to complement the vegetables, such as Marietta's Tuscan Roasted Chicken (page 209), and your dinner is all set. And for vegetarians, it's a winner all on its own.

INGREDIENTS
10 small red or white new potatoes, thinly sliced
2 small zucchini, thinly sliced
7 Roma tomatoes, thinly sliced
6 tbsp Parmesan cheese, freshly grated
1/3 cup packed fresh basil leaves, chopped
1/2 tsp dried thyme
1/2 tsp dried oregano
Olive oil
1/3 cup chicken or vegetable stock

METHOD
Preheat oven to 400°F. Line a 13x9-inch greased shallow casserole with alternate slices of potatoes, zucchini and tomatoes, using half the amount of each. Sprinkle with half the cheese and herbs; drizzle a little oil over all. Layer remaining portions, ending with the cheese and herbs. Pour chicken or vegetable stock over top. Bake for 40 to 45 minutes or until potatoes are tender.

PREPARATION TIME: 25 minutes

BULGUR RICE PILAF

SERVES 6

The combination of cracked bulgur wheat and brown rice spiked with turmeric and lemon gives this dish a unique flavour and nut-like texture. This recipe can be prepared the day ahead and reheated just before serving.

INGREDIENTS
2 tbsp butter
½ cup onion, finely chopped
½ cup uncooked bulgur wheat
½ cup brown rice, washed and strained
½ tsp turmeric
⅓ cup currants or raisins (optional)
Salt and pepper to taste
2 cups chicken stock, heated to boiling
2 tbsp parsley, chopped
Zest and juice of ½ lemon
⅓ cup toasted pecans, finely chopped (optional)
    (see Diane's secrets, page 91)

METHOD
Melt the butter in a large saucepan. Add onion, bulgur, brown rice and turmeric and sauté until golden, about 4 minutes. Add rest of ingredients except parsley, lemon zest and juice, and pecans. Simmer for 25 to 30 minutes, covered, until all the liquid is absorbed. Add the remaining ingredients; toss and serve. (If preparing ahead, refrigerate after simmering. To reheat, bake at 350°F for 25 to 30 minutes or until hot.)

PREPARATION TIME: 10 minutes

YAM AND BUTTERNUT SQUASH PURÉE

Butternut squash adds a slightly nutty taste to the sweetness of the yams in this tasty side dish. I always include this purée with my Christmas turkey.

INGREDIENTS

Olive or vegetable oil

4 lb medium yams, unpeeled

1 butternut squash (about 2 lb peeled), halved and seeded

¼ cup orange liqueur (optional)

2 tbsp butter

Pinch each of salt, pepper and nutmeg

⅓ cup toasted filberts or pecans, chopped (optional) (see Diane's secrets, page 91)

METHOD

Preheat the oven to 400°F. Rub a large cookie sheet with a little olive or vegetable oil. Place the yams on the sheet, along with the squash halves, cut side down. Roast about 1 hour until both are soft. Cool and peel, discarding the skin. Cut the yams and squash in large chunks and put into a food processor. Add the remaining ingredients except the nuts, and purée until creamy. Spoon into a greased 4- to 5-cup casserole. (Can be prepared up to this point and refrigerated for 1 or 2 days.)

When ready to serve, reheat at 400°F for 35 minutes, or until heated through, adding the nuts in the last 10 minutes.

Less fat: Leave out the butter.

PREPARATION TIME: 10 minutes plus roasting time

DIANE'S SECRETS

I always use the dark yams, rather than the lighter yellow sweet potatoes. I prefer their rich flavour and vivid orange colour. If butternut squash isn't available, you can add 3 or 4 more yams.

CHEF MICHAEL NOBLE'S MUSHROOM RISOTTO

SERVES 4

Michael Noble is the
executive chef of one of the
top restaurants in North
America, Diva at the Met,
in the Metropolitan Hotel in
Vancouver. He donates
his time freely to many
fundraising causes in
Vancouver. In 1998, I was
chair of the committee for
the Vancouver Canuck's
fundraising luncheon for the
Canuck Foundation and
other charities. I invited
Michael to be our celebrity
chef for the occasion, and he
happily accepted. The event
was a tremendous success.

One of the auction
items was a Tuscan dinner
for eight, hosted by Doug
and me at our home. I was
delighted when Chef Michael
offered to make his famous
Mushroom Risotto with us
that evening.

I am a great fan of risotto and Chef Michael's is magnifico! It's full of the wonderful flavours of the mushrooms, Parmesan cheese and fresh basil. And his Parmesan tuiles, or little cheese cups, complement the risotto perfectly. Double the recipe if you are a great fan of risotto!

INGREDIENTS
2 tbsp butter
¼ cup onion, diced
3 cloves garlic, chopped
¾ cup arborio rice
2 cups (approx.) chicken stock, heated
2 tbsp vegetable oil
½ medium portobello mushroom, sliced in pieces
½ cup shiitake mushrooms, sliced
1 cup chanterelle mushrooms (or any other kind of available mushroom), sliced
Salt and pepper to taste
1 tbsp butter
3 tbsp Parmesan cheese, grated
2 tbsp fresh basil, coarsely chopped
4 Parmesan Tuiles (see next page)

METHOD

In a medium-size saucepan, melt the 2 tbsp butter over moderate heat; sauté the onions and garlic until translucent. Add the rice and continue sautéeing 1 to 2 minutes, stirring constantly, until the rice is warm. Begin adding the hot chicken stock one ladle at a time. Continue stirring, keeping the rice at a constant simmer while adding more stock every couple of minutes to keep the risotto liquid. Cook 18 to 20 minutes or until the rice is *al dente* and the risotto is creamy. You may need to add more stock if it seems too dry.

While risotto is cooking, in a separate pan heat the vegetable oil and sauté the mushrooms on high until soft. Season with salt and pepper. Add the mushrooms to the rice during the last 5 to 8 minutes of cooking. When the rice is almost finished cooking, add the 1 tbsp butter, Parmesan cheese and basil. Spoon the risotto into the prepared Parmesan tuiles (see below) and serve.

PARMESAN TUILES

On silicon or parchment paper, spread 1 cup grated Reggiano Parmesan cheese to form 4 discs, each 3 inches in diameter. Bake for a few minutes at 375°F until the cheese melts and is golden brown. Remove from the oven and cool enough to handle. Place the cheese discs over inverted cups and let cool, so that when the cups are removed the baked cheese takes on their shape.

PREPARATION TIME: 60 minutes

DIANE'S SECRETS *Parmesan Reggiano is the best Italian Parmesan you can buy, and it's worth every penny!*

Former Vancouver Canuck players Scott Walker and Peter Zezel were my assistants in preparing the dinner. It was a riot to see these hockey players cooking with their huge hands as Chef Michael taught them the fine art of making the perfect risotto. The guests loved every minute of it! Scott and Peter were good sports, and Michael enjoyed coaching them in the kitchen. The guests cheered when Michael, Scott and Peter presented their "Canuck" risotto in magnificent Parmesan tuiles, topped with a sprig of rosemary. Then they raved as they tasted it. It was a winning performance for the risotto trio and a fun night for everyone. ☙

CHARMAINE'S FAST AND SPICY
ROVERETTO SPAGHETTI

SERVES 2

Charmaine Crooks was Canada's premier 400- and 800-metre runner during much of the eighties and nineties. She qualified for five Olympic Games from 1980 to 1996, and she was a finalist in the 400 metres in 1984 and won a silver medal as a member of the 1984 women's 4x400-metre relay team. She had the honour of carrying the Canadian flag in the opening ceremonies at the 1996 Atlanta Olympic Games. In 1999, Charmaine was appointed to the IOC Ethics Committee. She is now a motivational speaker and television host.

Doug has coached Charmaine since 1989, and we treasure our long friendship with her and her husband Anders Thorsen. When she has a spare moment to cook at home, her Italian spaghetti creation is Anders' most frequent request. This is how Charmaine describes it: "This recipe is inspired from a track meet in 1982 that our Canadian team attended in Roveretto, Italy. Diane and Doug were part of our team, along with their daughter Jennifer. When the team left for home, I was stuck in a little family-run hotel for a few extra days before going on to another competition. I had the chance to watch the hotel cook make this simple, easy pasta sauce. It's a real time and calorie saver!"

INGREDIENTS
1 lb spaghetti, cooked according to package directions, drained and tossed with a little olive oil and Parmesan cheese
1 can (28 oz) Italian Roma tomatoes
2 tbsp olive oil
3 large cloves garlic, crushed
¼ cup fresh basil leaves, cut into slivers
1 tbsp Parmesan cheese, freshly grated
Pinch each salt and pepper
1 tsp sugar
Dash Peri Peri sauce or Tabasco, or to taste

METHOD

Prepare the spaghetti and set aside. Drain the tomatoes, reserving the juice. Heat the olive oil in a fry pan. Add the garlic, sauté a few minutes, then slowly add the tomatoes, breaking into chunks with your hands. Add basil, Parmesan cheese, salt, pepper, sugar and Peri Peri sauce. Simmer for 10 minutes or until thickened slightly. If it becomes too thick, add a little of the reserved tomato juice.

Add the cooked spaghetti noodles to the pan and toss to coat. Serve immediately with additional Parmesan cheese.

PREPARATION TIME: 25 minutes

In 1987, the world championships for track and field were held in Rome, with athletic teams from over 165 nations. Among the participants was Charmaine Crooks, a finalist in the 4x400-metre relay. One of the highlights of the trip for Charmaine and me was to be invited to a private audience with Pope John Paul II at his summer retreat, Castel Gondolfo. As it turned out, it wasn't exactly private as there were about 900 invited guests!

On a blistering hot day, we arrived to be paraded through a very small garden gate for a security check. We were then herded into a grand hall with seating for everyone. The athletes were ushered to the back of the hall and the dignitaries sat up front. We sat in the hot auditorium for over an hour and a half, which made the athletes very restless. We had had a long bus ride to get there, and everyone was hungry and thirsty. Finally, the Pope appeared on stage and proceeded to speak in seven languages, welcoming the athletes to the world championships. Everyone was in awe as he spoke with such passion.

I had invited our Polish coach, Bogden Propawski, to come along with the athletes, and he was excited to see the Pope, who was also Polish-born, in person. When Pope John Paul II spoke in Polish, Bogden had tears streaming down his face. He turned to me and said, "Diane, I must be in heaven!" When the Pope finished his speech, he unexpectedly proceeded down the middle aisle. The security went wild as everyone rushed to be closer. Bogden and I ended up right on the aisle, and I stood on a chair as the Pope drew nearer. As he approached us, Bogden said something in Polish and Pope John Paul looked up at me, thinking I had spoken. He reached up and took my hand, and I looked him in the eyes and said the only thing I could think of, "Canada!" Still holding my hand, he replied, "Cannnadda!" I will never forget that moment in my life! By then, Bogden was crying his eyes out.

In our dining room that evening, Bogden told our entire team the story of our special meeting with his Pope from Poland, and Charmaine and I listened with joy! ♗

QUICK PASTA WITH CLAMS

SERVES 2

Once in a while I have the craving for pasta with a creamy clam sauce. This is my super-quick pasta dish, and it's super delicious, too!

Less fat: Eliminate the whipping cream or use half whipping cream and half light cream. Reduce the clam juice and wine to about ½ cup, and use vegetable or olive oil instead of the butter. With these substitutions, the sauce will be more broth-like, but still tasty.

INGREDIENTS
1 lb spaghetti or angel hair pasta
2 tbsp butter
3 large cloves garlic, finely chopped
¼ cup onion, finely chopped
Pinch red pepper flakes
Salt and pepper to taste
1 can (10- to 12-oz) baby clams with juice
1 ½ cups whipping cream
¼ cup dry white wine
Juice of ½ lemon
1 cup Parmesan cheese

METHOD
Cook the pasta according to package directions. While the pasta is cooking, melt the butter in a large fry pan. Add the garlic, onion, pepper flakes, salt and pepper, and sauté until golden. Add the clams and their juices, whipping cream, wine and lemon juice. Let simmer to thicken and reduce on low heat, stirring frequently.

Drain the pasta and toss with a few tablespoons of the Parmesan cheese. Add the pasta to the clam sauce and toss. Serve immediately with remaining Parmesan cheese and French bread to soak up the sauce.

PREPARATION TIME: 10 minutes

BARBECUE KIWI LAMB KEBABS

SERVES 6

In 1986, Doug and I were invited by our international athletics federation, the IAAF, to be part of a travelling coaching team from Canada and Australia touring New Zealand. I gave lectures on foods for optimum performance for Olympic athletes, and Doug and the other invited coaches held clinics. We were all entertained royally by our New Zealand hosts. In particular, they threw many fabulous New Zealand lamb barbecues. Several years later, I received this recipe for a unique marinade for barbecued lamb from the New Zealand Beef and Lamb Marketing Bureau. This recipe meets the National Heart Foundation Creative Cuisine guidelines, designed to promote a healthier diet.

DIANE'S SECRETS

These kebabs go well with a simple Greek salad, tzatziki and pita bread.

INGREDIENTS
1 kiwi fruit
2 cloves garlic, crushed
2 tbsp dark soy sauce
2 tbsp dry sherry
1 tbsp olive or vegetable oil
½ tsp sugar
Pepper to taste
2 lb lamb (lean leg or shoulder), cut in ¾-inch cubes
12 very long, strong bushy stems of fresh rosemary

METHOD
Scoop out the flesh from the kiwi fruit and mash in a bowl until smooth. Mix in all other ingredients except the lamb and rosemary. Add the cubed lamb and stir. Marinate at room temperature for about 20 minutes (maximum 1 hour). (The kiwi fruit acts as a tenderizer and if mixed with meat for several hours it will make it too soft.) Drain the lamb.

Remove the leaves from two-thirds of the rosemary leaving a little bushy top, thinning out if too thick. Thread equal amount of lamb on each rosemary "skewer," and grill for 5 to 7 minutes, turning skewer to brown meat on all sides. Do not overcook.

PREPARATION TIME: 1 hour

GRILLED CHICKEN WITH RED PEPPER CHUTNEY

SERVES 6

In the mid-eighties, I was invited to a special luncheon at the Four Seasons Hotel in Vancouver, prepared by the executive chef and a guest chef from California's Mondavi Winery. This recipe is my adaptation of the light chicken dish that was served. The marinade is what we use for our Tomato Café chicken breasts, without the lemon zest and herbs.

In the early eighties, one of the most avant-garde restaurants to open in Vancouver was Jackie's in the Kerrisdale neighbourhood. The walls looked like black patent leather, and the round tables were covered with French floral prints. It was elegant, and it was the place to be seen.

The general manager was a young man, Ruy Paes-Braga. He is now the regional vice-president and general manager of the Four Seasons Hotel in Vancouver. Ruy has had a most distinguished career in the hotel industry and has won many honours from his peers. He gives generously to many fundraisers, from medical research to the arts. Doug and I have been a small part of the special Heart and Stroke Foundation breakfasts held at the Four Seasons each year to raise funds for research in this field. Vancouver is fortunate to have Ruy Paes-Braga and his Four Season's team so dedicated to giving back to our community. &

INGREDIENTS
6 whole chicken breasts, boned, skinned and halved

MARINADE
½ cup lemon juice
1 tbsp lemon zest, finely chopped
2 tbsp Dijon mustard
¼ cup mixed herbs (fresh rosemary, thyme, basil, oregano and parsley, or a combination of any you wish)
Pepper to taste

RED PEPPER CHUTNEY
4 large tomatoes, peeled, seeded and chopped
3 red peppers, grilled, peeled and chopped
6 tbsp raspberry vinegar
4 tbsp white sugar

METHOD

Place chicken breasts in a single layer in a glass dish. Combine the marinade ingredients and pour over the chicken breasts. Cover and refrigerate for 2 to 4 hours.

Meanwhile, prepare the chutney. In a small fry pan, mix the vinegar and sugar and cook until it starts to form a thin syrup and the sugar begins to caramelize. Add the tomatoes and red peppers. Stir to blend, and simmer on low until slightly thickened. Set aside.

Grill the chicken breasts on the barbecue or under the broiler for about 6 to 8 minutes on each side, or until cooked and no pink juices show. Serve with the red pepper chutney.

PREPARATION TIME: 15 minutes

DIANE'S SECRETS

The red pepper chutney is best made the day of serving and kept at room temperature. Reheat slightly before serving. It is refreshing, tart and tasty, and it goes well with grilled fish, too.

Back in the early eighties, I remember doing a class at Tools and Techniques Kitchen Boutique in West Vancouver and whipping up red pepper chutney. Having done many classes in their kitchen, I knew exactly where everything was. So when I grabbed the jar of sugar from the counter and added it to the chutney, I never stopped to check if it was actually sugar! When the chutney wasn't caramelizing after several minutes, I knew something was wrong. Lo and behold, it tasted totally salty. I found out that the staff had done a total reorganization of the kitchen the day before, and someone forgot to label the salt and sugar jars, standing side by side! Now, I always taste first before adding sugar or salt!

I calmly rinsed the peppers and tomatoes several times to remove the salt. All the stores were closed, so I had to salvage the chutney from what I had. However, the students were very understanding and endured the particularly salty chutney. An extra glass of wine was welcomed that evening!

CAMPBELL RIVER GRILLED SALMON

SERVES 6

In 1982, Bob and Jacquie Gordon invited me to an unbelievable salmon barbecue in Campbell River on my final book tour for *Chef on the Run*. This recipe comes from the First Nations chief in Campbell River, who shared his special secret ingredients for the most succulent salmon I have ever eaten. The combination of soy sauce, brown sugar and a hint of whisky gives the salmon its slightly smoked flavour. I won't do salmon any other way!

INGREDIENTS
One large salmon fillet with skin on (about 2½ lbs)
   or 6 salmon fillet steaks, about 4½ oz each
½ cup vegetable oil
2 tbsp soy sauce
1 tsp fresh garlic, crushed, or 1 tbsp garlic powder
Pepper to taste
¼ cup rye whisky
2 tbsp brown sugar

METHOD
Wipe the fish and set aside. Combine the rest of the ingredients to make the marinade. Pour marinade over the fish, reserving some for basting, and leave it to steep for about 2 hours. Barbecue on oiled grill 3 to 4 minutes per side, just until the fish flakes. Brush with the remaining marinade several times during cooking. Serve with wedges of lemon.

PREPARATION TIME: 2 to 3 hours, including marinating salmon

QUICK CHEDDAR-CHEESE BREAD

Another quick loaf that never fails! Try substituting the Cheddar cheese with Parmesan, fontina or whatever you wish. I like to pop a loaf in the oven for Sunday brunch; it goes so well with any egg dish.

INGREDIENTS
2 cups all-purpose flour
4 tsp baking powder
¼ tsp salt
¼ cup butter
1 ⅓ cup grated sharp Cheddar cheese, divided
¼ cup softened sun-dried tomatoes, chopped
    (optional)
2 eggs
¼ cup granulated sugar
1 cup milk

METHOD
Sift the flour, baking powder and salt together into a bowl. Cut in butter until mixture resembles small peas. Add 1 cup cheese and the sun-dried tomatoes; toss.

In another bowl, beat the eggs until fluffy. Gradually add the sugar. Stir in the milk. Add egg mixture to dry ingredients. Blend just to combine.

Pour into a greased 8x4-inch loaf pan. Sprinkle the remaining ⅓ cup cheese evenly on top of the batter. Press down slightly. Bake at 350°F for 50 to 60 minutes or until a toothpick inserted in the middle comes out clean. Remove from pan and cool.

Serve hot or cold, thinly sliced. Keeps 2 to 3 days well wrapped.

PREPARATION TIME: 10 minutes

LESLEY STOWE'S GRAHAM BREAD

MAKES 1 LOAF

Lesley Stowe, one of Vancouver's most talented chefs, graduated in the early eighties from La Varenne Cooking School in Paris and proceeded to head up the catering and take-out division of The Salt Box kitchen boutique, located in Vancouver's Arbutus Village. Joyce Perkes, Liz McKenzie and Becky Paris Turner were running The Salt Box at the time and wanted to complement their thriving store with a take-out and catering establishment. Lesley brought in my friend Barbara Watts to assist her. The two of them eventually started cooking classes at The Wise Owl china store in Vancouver, where I taught for many years. Lesley has gone on to open one of the top speciality food and catering establishments in Canada, Lesley Stowe Fine Foods.

This graham bread is a Maritime recipe that was popular at The Salt Box, and one that my students always raved about in my cooking classes. It's for anyone who shudders at the thought of making yeast breads! I make my loaves in Crisco shortening tins, or large juice tins, but Lesley would make them in small loaf pans. This recipe is created specifically for baking in tins. Loaves will keep for 2 to 3 days well wrapped.

INGREDIENTS
2 tbsp brown sugar
½ tsp baking soda
1 tbsp baking powder
½ tsp salt
⅓ cup skim milk powder
1 cup all-purpose flour
2 cups graham flour
1 ¾ cups water

METHOD

Combine all the ingredients except water, stirring to blend well. Add water and stir just to mix. Grease a clean 2-lb juice or shortening tin well and pour in the bread mix. Seal top with greased aluminum foil. Bake in a 350°F oven for about 1½ hours. Do not peek!

Remove loaf from the tin immediately when done. It should sound hollow when you tap the bottom. Cool and wrap in foil. Slice paper thin to serve.

PREPARATION TIME: 10 minutes

 DIANE'S SECRETS

This bread is great as the base for open-faced sandwiches of shaved ham and mustard relish, or just toasted with homemade jam.

OLIVE MARTINI LOAF

MAKES 1 LOAF

Nippy and crunchy, this bread, which uses gin, vodka or vermouth along with sour olives, adds a "spike" to salads and soups. Tuck an extra loaf into the freezer for emergencies. Great with martinis, too!

INGREDIENTS
2⅔ cups all-purpose flour
1 tbsp baking powder
Pinch salt
2 tbsp white sugar
5 tbsp butter
1 large egg
¼ cup liquid from olives
1 cup whole milk
¼ cup gin, vodka or vermouth
¼ cup Parmesan cheese, freshly grated
½ cup toasted pecans or walnuts, finely
  chopped (see Diane's secrets, page 91)
1 cup whole pimiento-stuffed olives, drained

METHOD
Blend the flour, baking powder, salt and sugar in a mixing bowl. Cut in the butter and blend well. In a separate bowl, beat egg, olive liquid, milk, gin and cheese. Add to the flour mixture and gently blend together. Fold in the nuts and olives. Batter will be thick.

Turn into a well-greased 9x5-inch loaf pan and bake at 350°F for 45 to 55 minutes, or until a toothpick inserted in the middle comes out clean. Cool. Loaf will keep fresh for 2 days and freezes well. Serve thinly sliced.

PREPARATION TIME: 10 minutes

 DIANE'S SECRETS *Make this loaf a day ahead or time to allow the flavours to peak.*

BANANA ICE WITH RASPBERRY PURÉE

SERVES 4 TO 6

I always keep ripe bananas in our freezer so I can quickly whip up a smooth, creamy, low-cal banana ice cream. Children of all ages love making this unbelievable ice cream. It's right up there with the richest commercial brands. The difference is that there's no heavy cream or egg yolks. Just remember to prepare it right before serving as it doesn't freeze well.

INGREDIENTS
5 or 6 large, ripe bananas, frozen
3 to 4 tbsp low-fat vanilla or fruit yogurt
Raspberry Purée (see page 157)
Raspberries or strawberries, frozen or fresh
    (optional)
Fresh mint (optional)

METHOD
Cut the frozen bananas into ½-inch slices and blend in a food processor with the yogurt until smooth and creamy. If bananas stick to the bottom of the processor, stop and stir occasionally.

Put one generous scoop in each dessert dish. Drizzle a little Raspberry Purée over the top and garnish with berries and mint.

PREPARATION TIME: 10 minutes

DIANE'S SECRETS

When fresh berries are in season, I often add a few strawberries to the bananas for a banana-strawberry ice cream.

MARCELLE'S LOW-FAT TUSCAN CHEESECAKE

We first met Marcelle and Don McLean and their daughter Jennifer in 1985. They had one of the top television commercial production companies in Canada. They were looking for a food stylist, and I was recommended by *Western Living* magazine. We spent many years of joy creating food layouts for commercials, and we became close family friends.

When we opened our Tomato-To-Go take-out division, Marcelle agreed to come aboard as manager. We both had a particular fondness for sweets, until she was diagnosed as diabetic. Marcelle then began producing some fantastic desserts, coffeecakes and cheesecakes, not only for herself, but for our customers requesting low-fat, no-sugar choices. When *Appeal* magazine was launched for the Save-On-Foods grocery stores in 1998, I was invited to do a feature on healthy eating. I took high-fat classic dishes and turned them into tasty and healthy dishes. Marcelle's Low-Fat Tuscan Cheesecake was the sensational grand finale.

INGREDIENTS

CRUST
1 cup Graham wafer or other cookie crumbs
3 tbsp liquid honey, or ¼ cup fruit concentrate
½ tsp almond extract
¼ cup toasted hazelnuts, chopped (see Diane's secrets, page 91)

FILLING
1 package (9 oz) Philadelphia light cream cheese
2 cups 1% cottage cheese
½ cup fat-free sour cream
½ cup liquid honey or 1 cup fruit concentrate
2 tbsp espresso or instant coffee powder, diluted in ¼ cup warm 1% milk
3 egg whites
2 tbsp flour
1 tbsp vanilla

METHOD

CRUST

Preheat the oven to 350°F. Mix together the crust ingredients until the mixture is evenly moistened. Pat evenly into the bottom and up the sides (about ½-inch high) of a greased 9-inch springform pan. (Use the back of a spoon dipped in orange juice to make the spreading easier). Bake for 10 minutes. Set aside.

FILLING

In a food processor, blend together all ingredients until smooth. Pour into prepared crust and bake in 350°F oven for 65 to 75 minutes, or until set in the middle. Make sure the middle is not too soft before taking cake out of the oven. Cool, then loosen edges with a round-tipped knife; refrigerate overnight before serving.

To serve, top with Raspberry Purée (see below).

PREPARATION TIME: 20 minutes.

DIANE'S SECRETS

Fruit concentrate is available in health food stores. Don't be surprised at how long it takes to bake this cheesecake compared to others; there is a lot more liquid in this light version and it requires more baking. If you prefer a lemon cheesecake, substitute the juice and rind of two lemons for the espresso coffee.

RASPBERRY PURÉE

In a food processor or blender, purée 2 cups fresh or frozen unsweetened raspberries, then strain in a fine mesh strainer. Add a little sugar, if desired. If desired, you can use strawberries. This purée can be made ahead and frozen. Thaw at room temperature for about 2 hours or overnight in the refrigerator. It will keep in the refrigerator for several days.

HOT APRICOT SOUFFLÉ WITH MANGO PURÉE

SERVES 4 TO 6

Apricots and mangoes star in this elegant, light and easy-to-make soufflé. I bake it in a 1-quart soufflé dish, which allows it to rise well above the rim.

INGREDIENTS
6 oz dried apricots
1 cup unsweetened apricot nectar
1 tsp vanilla
6 large egg whites, at room temperature
Pinch salt
½ tsp cream of tartar
2 tbsp fine granulated sugar or fructose
Mango Purée (see page 159)
2 kiwi fruit, peeled and thinly sliced

METHOD
Spray the soufflé dish with non-stick vegetable spray. Make a 3-inch collar of aluminum foil and secure it around dish. Spray inside of the collar.

In a small saucepan, cook the apricots with nectar for 15 minutes or until tender. Cool and purée in a food processor or blender. Add the vanilla and blend (mixture will be thick). Set aside.

Heat the oven to 375°F. (If you have made the apricot base in advance and refrigerated it, bring it to room temperature while you prepare the eggs.) Beat the egg whites until frothy, then add the salt and cream of tartar. Beat until slightly stiff, but still glossy. Add the sugar a little at a time and beat until stiff. Fold in a little of the apricot mixture, then add the rest very gently until well blended. Pour into the soufflé dish; it should fill the dish to just above the rim. Bake for 25 to 30 minutes until golden and firm to the touch. Remove the foil and serve immediately with Mango Purée and sliced kiwi fruit.

MANGO PURÉE

Peel, seed and chop three fresh ripe mangoes. In a food processor or blender, purée until smooth. Refrigerate until ready to use. Makes about ½ cup. If fresh mangoes aren't available, substitute 1 can (14 oz) mangoes, drained.

PREPARATION TIME: 30 minutes

Like all cooked soufflés, this must be baked immediately before serving, but you can have the base ready, whip up the egg whites at the last minute, and pop it in the oven while you're eating your main course.

JANE'S CHOCOLATE POUND CAKE

SERVES 10 TO 12

Close friends of ours, Jane and Gerry Swan, have been active in track and field for as long as we have. In the eighties, their Valley Royals track and field club in Abbotsford, British Columbia, was going strong, and it continues to be one of the top clubs in Canada. Gerry still coaches middle distances, and Jane has served as chairman of B.C. Athletics. They have hosted many national competitions in Abbotsford, and Jane puts on quite a feast for the athletes and officials afterwards. Her chocolate pound cake has become famous! It's light, almost melts in your mouth and is a must with summer berries. It's better than any pound cake I've ever tried at high tea in Great Britain, and it often disappears even before it reaches the buffet table!

INGREDIENTS
1½ cups shortening
3 cups granulated sugar
½ cup Dutch cocoa
4 extra-large eggs
2¾ cups all-purpose flour
½ tsp baking powder
¼ tsp salt
1¼ cups milk
1 tbsp vanilla

METHOD
In large mixing bowl, cream the shortening with the sugar and cocoa. Add the eggs one at a time, beating after each addition. Add the dry ingredients alternately with the milk, adding the vanilla before the last portion of dry ingredients. Mix until blended. Don't overbeat!

Pour into a greased and floured angel-cake tube pan. Bake at 325°F for about 1¾ hours, or until the middle bounces back and a skewer inserted in the middle comes out clean.

PREPARATION TIME: 15 minutes

In 1986, the Commonwealth Games were held in Edinburgh, Scotland, and once again I was one of the team managers and Doug was coaching his athletes. During the Games, the Queen invited all the Commonwealth athletes and officials to a Royal Garden Party at Holyrood Castle, the Royal family's summer residence.

The team was excited as we wandered through the massive castle gardens. Royal bands were playing, wine was flowing freely, and English tea sandwiches were being served. Yellow-and-white striped tents were scattered throughout the royal grounds with tables laden with teatime treats. It was very festive, with all the athletes and officials of the Commonwealth wearing their official blazers and our Canadian red uniforms adding a colourful backdrop. A few of the athletes and I quickly took note that six of the royal family were in attendance: Queen Elizabeth, Prince Philip, Diana, Princess of Wales, Prince Charles, Princess Anne and Prince Edward. The only two absent were Sarah, Duchess of York and Prince Andrew, who were on their honeymoon!

Three athletes and I decided to watch the two royal Scottish guards assigned to each member of the royal family. The pattern was for one guard to lead the royal member and one to stay a little distance behind as they moved freely talking to the athletes and officials. We decided to see if we could manage to speak to all six of the royal family. We would rush in front of the royal guard and stand waiting for the royal member to walk right into us.

Well, it worked! Each member of the royal family would stop right in front of us and strike up a conversation with each of us. What was impressive was that they actually attempted to indulge in a true conversation, looking us right in the eye and taking an interest in hearing about our team and whether we were enjoying the Games. We came away feeling fortunate, sensing that we would never have the opportunity to be a part of such a royal garden party again. So right we were! &

The Explosive

Vegetables and Side Dishes

Main Courses

Breads and Cereals

Desserts

The Explosive Nineties

IN THE EIGHTIES, THE HEADLINE IN A MAJOR MAGAZINE ARTICLE DECLARED, "Women in the eighties have it all!" We had blossoming careers and busy families. We entertained often, worked out to keep fit, decorated our homes and volunteered time to many social causes. If we had it "all" in the eighties, then in the nineties, we'd had enough! The headlines changed and read instead, "I am Woman, I am invincible, I am EXHAUSTED!"

In the nineties the wake-up call on health issues and family values was even greater than in the eighties. The baby boomers were hitting middle age and looking for the right balance in their everyday living. I think we all took a hard look at what we valued most in our lives, and the bottom line was that the most important things were our health, family and friends.

Of all the decades, for me the nineties felt like running a 100-metre dash! It was an explosive, challenging and fast-moving decade. Doug and I travelled – and ate – our way around many countries of world. We attended the Commonwealth Games in Auckland in 1990 as spectators. In the spring of 1992, my twin brother, David, and his wife Dianne, joined Doug and me on a whirl-wind trip to Paris and parts of Provence. They joined us again in 1996, along with 16 other food aficionados, at Umberto Menghi's amazing Villa Delia in the Tuscan region of Italy for a week of cooking classes and touring the ancient Italian villages and Florence. In 1994 we had the honour of being the "co-mayors" of the athletes' village during the Commonwealth Games in Victoria, British Columbia. In 1996 we attended the Olympic Games in Atlanta. Doug was coaching Charmaine Crooks, Canada's 800-metre champion, and before the Games opened, we took the opportunity to enjoy the warm southern U.S. hospitality and cuisine as we travelled throughout Florida, South Carolina and Georgia. In 1997 we travelled to Spain and Portugal, and in 1998 we spent a month on the tropical island of Maui. We also hosted lifestyle cruises to Alaska, the Mexican Riviera and the Caribbean for the B.C. Automobile Association from 1995 to 1998.

Throughout all of our travels in the nineties, what I remember most are the times we spent dining in little bistros and cafés, just watching and observing the other patrons. Language was never an issue; everyone took part in the simple enjoyment of the food and wines of that particular country. In most cases, we found the waiters and staff to be hospitable and patient, explaining their specialities to us. They took pride in their ethnic heritage and made us feel welcome.

Of course, when I think back to the nineties, the restaurant that sticks out most in my mind is our own Tomato Fresh Food Café, which we opened in 1991 with our daughter, Jennifer, and two other partners, Jamie Norris and Haik

Gharibians. Since then, Haik has passed away, and Jamie has moved on to concentrate on his writing, and we now have a new partner on board, Christian Gaudreault.

As I meander through our family restaurant and observe our customers, I get the same warm feeling that Doug and I have experienced at restaurants throughout the world. It is truly one of the great passions of the world, sharing good times over a glass of wine and a tasty meal, no matter what language is spoken. We all look forward to visiting restaurants to celebrate special events, an anniversary, birthday or a new romance, or as tourists experiencing the cuisine of another country. And what I observed in restaurants throughout the world in the nineties is that people were once again seeking "comfort" foods, and family dining reigned supreme. From banana bread to macaroni and cheese done "nineties-style," everyone was looking for traditional, simple cooking once again. We had come full circle, back to the home cooking of the fifties. Even in haute cuisine establishments, where the presentations may have been elegant and tiered mile-high on the plates, the tastes were pure and uncomplicated.

It was this renewed interest in simple home cooking that made entertaining at home more popular than ever in the nineties. New houses, condos and apartments were designed with the living space centred on the family room, with everything from the computer station, television, kitchen and dining table all rolled into one room. Everyone could pitch in and help prepare a meal while chatting about the day's activities. Older homes were being remodelled with more emphasis on the family room as the heart of the home.

Farmers' markets were thriving in the nineties, and organic or hot house produce gained popularity. Fresh herbs were readily available, and many of us took pride in creating our own herb gardens. The intensity of flavours was stepped up a notch or two, and our tastebuds exploded with what was hyped as "fusion" dishes, with any combination of ethnic ingredients coming together in one dish. Many coined it "confusion," but it did teach us that we could be more adventuresome in our cooking!

Cookbook and lifestyle book sales also exploded in the nineties. In 1990 my fourth book, *Fresh Chef on the Run*, was released, and in 1995, Raincoast Books published the wild tales and recipes of our Tomato Café, *Diane Clement at the*

In the early nineties, I became involved with BC Hot House when they launched their Juicy Secrets campaign. My role was to develop new recipes for their superior produce: tomatoes, peppers, cucumbers and butter lettuce. My recipes are now available on their popular web site and on recipe cards printed and distributed for promotional purposes. I act as their spokesperson, doing cooking demonstrations throughout Lower Mainland venues, including VanDusen Gardens, Granville Island Market and at Chinese New Year celebrations. I periodically appear on radio and television. It's been a great experience for me, and I continue to enjoy my affiliation with BC Hot House.

Tomato. Other B.C. chefs and celebrities joined the cookbook scene. Umberto Menghi, John Bishop, Caren McSherry Valagao, Karen Barnaby, James Barber, Jurgen Gothe and Vicki Gabereau all produced cookbooks that made the Canadian best-seller list. Then eight vibrant, talented Vancouver women chefs collaborated on yet another best-seller, *The Girls Who Dish*, published in 1998. There was no shortage of Vancouver culinary talents revealing their recipe secrets! British Columbia's chefs led the way in showing the rest of Canada that we love entertaining and cooking, West Coast style!

Television and radio food shows also gained international top ratings, with *Emeril Live* and *The Two Fat Ladies* topping the charts on the new Food Network. Locally, I became involved with the BCTV's *Saturday Chef* series, appeared with Vicki Gabereau on CBC radio food shows, and later cooked up a storm on her new TV show, Global's *Vicki Gabereau Live*. The message was loud and clear: food enthusiasts wanted to learn more about cooking in their own kitchens. They were eager to find out the latest secrets from celebrity chefs.

Throughout the nineties I had the opportunity to cook and learn from many of these innovative chefs. The star chefs, who taught me that excellence is achieved only by motivation and desire to be the best that you can be, are B.C. chefs Umberto Menghi, John Bishop, Michael Noble, Sinclair Philip and Bernard Casavant. Lesley Stowe and Linda Meinhardt lead the way in offering Vancouverites gourmet food establishments comparable to the best in the world. Caren McSherry Valagao and her husband José spearheaded one of the top specialty food import businesses in Canada, Continental Importers. All of these people have been instrumental in Vancouver becoming recognized and honoured as one of the top cities in the world for restaurants and hospitality. In the meantime, throughout Canada local restaurants received accolades and top reviews, from *Gourmet* magazine to the prestigious Zagat restaurant ratings. Canadian chefs were finally recognized as being among the best in the world.

It wasn't easy to pick the best recipes of the nineties for this chapter – there were so many to choose from. Recipes from chefs during our many travels (Villa Delia's Melanzane-Riepieni, page 195), recipes from chefs I've worked with on television or at fundraising events (John Bishop's Maple Syrup Ice Cream, page 228), our own Tomato Café creations (David Alsop's Whisky Marinated Arctic Char with Tomato Chutney, page 216) and many old family classics made new (Margaret's Banana Bread, page 219) are all included in the pages that follow.

Judging from the forecasts of the experts on nutrition and exercise, the nineties' trend of preparing fresh, healthy home cooking, exercising more and finding the right balance in life will continue to be most people's lifestyle goals in the new millennium. I am excited to share the "best of the best of the nineties" with you. I hope that you will derive much pleasure from creating these dishes in your own kitchen for your family and friends!

CRILLON LE BRAVE APERITIF

SERVES 1

In 1992, this refreshing aperitif was the signature drink at the charming hilltop restaurant and hotel, Crillon le Brave, in the town of Crillon in Provence, France.

INGREDIENTS
4 oz fresh grapefruit juice
2 oz muscat wine
1 oz sweet sherry

METHOD
Mix ingredients to blend. Chill and serve in champagne flutes.

PREPARATION TIME: 5 minutes

DIANE'S SECRETS

Multiply the quantities as required for more servings. Refrigerate until ready to serve. You can make a large batch several hours before serving so that it is well chilled.

BLACK TURTLE BEAN SOUP • 132

Plate # 18 & *Zest for Life*

VEGETABLE GRATIN • 138

Plate # 20 ❧ *Zest for Life*

FRENCH ITALIAN TOMATO-BOCCONCINI TART • 170

Plate # 22 ❧ *Zest for Life*

Plate # 26   *Zest for Life*

Zest for Life   *Plate # 27*

CHRISTIAN'S SEARED SCALLOPS WITH MADRAS CURRY SAUCE AND CORN PUDDING • 214

Plate # 28 ❧ *Zest for Life*

DAVID'S WHISKY MARINATED ARCTIC CHAR WITH TOMATO CHUTNEY • 216

Zest for Life & *Plate # 29*

ME AND MY DAUGHTER JENNIFER SITTING DOWN TO ENJOY THE TORTILLA DE POTATAS • PAGE 204

Plate # 32 ❧ *Zest for Life*

THE WHAMMY!

This fruit drink is one of the most popular juices at our Tomato Café. It's known as "a tropical paradise"!

INGREDIENTS
1 ripe banana
1 cup orange juice, freshly squeezed
1 cup pineapple juice, preferably fresh

METHOD
In a blender or juicer, blend ingredients until smooth.

PREPARATION TIME: 3 minutes

DIANE'S SECRETS

Christian Gaudreault, our general manager and partner at the Tomato, is our wine expert and, to the delight of our customers, is always looking to increase our wine selection. In the summer of 1999, Christian recommended that we extend our liquor licence to include hard liquors, mainly to have special juicy cocktails with our fresh juices. Jennifer and I thought it was a super idea, and so did our customers!
By adding a good shot of rum to the fruit ingredients in this recipe, the Whammy! became Whammy Wow! on our special cocktail menu. And you will say "Wow!" after you taste it!

FRENCH ITALIAN TOMATO-BOCCONCINI TART

SERVES 6

This light tart celebrates my travels with Doug to both France and Italy during the nineties. The combination of the cheeses of both countries, the Dijon mustard of France, the ripe sweetness of perfect tomatoes and the taste of sweet basil makes this a winner of an appetizer. You can also serve it with a side salad for a light lunch.

INGREDIENTS

CRUST
1½ cups all-purpose flour
6 tbsp butter
2 tbsp vegetable oil
Pinch salt
7 tbsp ice water

FILLING
3 tbsp grainy or regular Dijon Mustard (approx.)
1 cup grated Gruyère or Emmentaler cheese
3 tbsp softened sun-dried tomatoes, chopped and
    blended with 1 tbsp olive oil
5 to 6 Roma tomatoes, thinly sliced and seeded
5 to 6 small bocconcini cheese balls, thinly sliced
2 tbsp fresh basil, chopped

METHOD

CRUST

Blend all ingredients quickly in a food processor. Wrap and refrigerate until firm, about 15 minutes. (Can be made a day or two ahead. Also freezes well.)

Roll out very thin, about ¼ inch. Fit into a 12-inch tart or pizza pan. Prick generously and bake at 425°F for 10 to 12 minutes or until slightly golden. (Can be baked a day or two ahead. Cover and refrigerate, or leave at room temperature.)

FILLING

In the baked pie shell, spread the mustard in a thin layer. Sprinkle the cheese and the sun-dried tomatoes over top. Overlap the fresh tomatoes and bocconcini slices. Bake at 350°F for 15 minutes or until the cheese is slightly melted and the tart is warm. Sprinkle with the basil, cut into wedges and serve. (The tart can be assembled 1 or 2 hours before serving and left at room temperature before baking.)

PREPARATION TIME: 15 minutes

CARAMELIZED ONION-CHÈVRE TART

What a combination: caramelized onions, fresh thyme and chèvre in a paper-thin crust! The caramelized onions can be served as a condiment as well with seafood and meats, or try them in a sandwich.

INGREDIENTS
1 pie crust (use Tomato-Bocconcini Tart recipe, page 170)
2 tbsp butter
¼ cup light olive oil
6 large, sweet white onions, peeled
2 tbsp freshly chopped thyme, or 2 tsp dried
1 tbsp sugar
Pinch each salt and pepper
1 cup crumbled chèvre or Gorgonzola cheese
Fresh thyme sprigs

METHOD

Prepare pie crust (see page 171). Cut the onions in half and slice paper thin. (A food processor slicer works well.) In a large fry pan, heat the butter and olive oil over medium heat to melt butter. Add the onions, thyme, sugar, salt and pepper. Simmer for about 40 to 45 minutes, stirring frequently, until the onions are golden brown and slightly caramelized. Do not over brown. Set aside. Cool, then refrigerate. Can be made a day or two ahead.

Preheat the oven to 400°F. Spread the onion mixture evenly over the crust. Sprinkle an even layer of the cheese over top. Bake 25 to 30 minutes, or until the crust is golden brown and the onions are warmed and the cheese melted. Slice into thin wedges or small squares. Garnish with thyme sprigs.

PREPARATION TIME: 1 hour

DIANE'S SECRETS

The onion filling freezes well. I often double the recipe and freeze the "onion marmalade," as it is often called, in 1-cup containers. It's a great base with sandwiches or grilled meats. Adding about 1 tbsp of balsamic vinegar to the mixture before you simmer it gives the marmalade a zing. Try it!

NEW WAVE PIQUANT THAI PRAWN DIP

SERVES 4

During the 1996 Olympic Games, Charmaine Crooks had the honour of carrying the Canadian flag for our Canadian Olympic team at the opening ceremonies. Consequently, CBC Television requested an interview with her later that week. She invited her husband, Anders, Doug and me to join her at the CNN host media centre so that we could all enjoy some of the nightly entertainment afterwards in the surrounding park. Charmaine mentioned our late-night plans to the interviewer, Don McLean, but as it turned out, by the time the interview was over it was near midnight, so we decided to immediately return to the Olympic Village and forego the walk.

As we were nearing our hotel, Anders's cell phone rang. It was his mother in a panic. "Anders, it's so good to hear your voice, are you all okay? There's been a terrible bombing at the CNN park, and there are people lying everywhere. Your Dad and I were horrified that you, Charmaine, Doug and Diane were there!"

During our time in the southern states, en route to the 1996 Atlanta Olympic Games, we visited our niece Diana and her husband, Doug Stofel, in Charleston, South Carolina. Diana loves to cook and she served this prawn dip, which has a hint of the Orient with the Chinese chili sauce, along with a touch of the South with the addition of fresh mint.

INGREDIENTS
1 tbsp cornstarch
1 tbsp cold water
¾ cup tomato sauce
Zest of 1 lime
¼ cup lime juice
3 tbsp brown sugar
1 tbsp Chinese sweet chili sauce
1 clove garlic, crushed
1 tbsp fresh mint, chopped
1 lb cooked, peeled medium prawns with tail on (about 24)

METHOD

Combine the cornstarch and water; set aside. In a small saucepan, combine remaining ingredients except prawns. Bring to a boil and add cornstarch mixture. Stir over medium heat until thickened slightly. Refrigerate.

To serve, pour dipping sauce in bowl; surround with prawns.

PREPARATION TIME: 15 minutes

DIANE'S SECRETS

I like to make the sauce a day ahead for the flavours to peak. I use commercial canned tomato sauce, as the texture and taste is perfect for this particular dip, but you can use your own or some from a deli, if you wish.

Vancouver had heard the news before we did! They had seen Charmaine's interview telling Don that the four of us were going to wander through the CNN Park exactly at the time the bomb went off! Little did Doug and I realize that our children were watching the interview as well and had been frantically waiting to hear from us.

The next day at the Olympic Stadium, a young man on a pair of crutches was sitting beside the four of us. He told us that he had been a few feet from the stage where the bomb went off. He had been injured, but not too badly. He told us the story and exclaimed, "I'm one of the lucky ones; I'm alive!" The four of us looked at each other and nodded, "So are we!" Luck was definitely with us that night.

PORTOBELLO MUSHROOM PIZZETA WITH PARMESAN AND PEPPERS

If wild mushrooms were the "royal" item in the nineties, the king of the family was the portobello. Vegetarians and other mushroom fans enjoyed grilled portobello steak as if they were eating a huge T-bone or ribs! Here is a fun way to present this "mucho grande" mushroom. It's also a perfect side dish for barbecued dishes.

INGREDIENTS
1 cup dry bread crumbs
½ cup freshly grated Parmesan cheese, divided
2 tbsp soft butter
2 cloves garlic, crushed
2 tbsp parsley, finely chopped
Pinch salt
Pepper to taste
¼ cup red and yellow peppers, finely chopped
4 whole portobello caps, about 4 inches in diameter
Olive oil
½ cup balsamic vinegar

METHOD
Preheat the oven to 350°F. In a small bowl, combine the bread crumbs, ¼ cup Parmesan cheese, butter, garlic, parsley, salt, pepper, and red and yellow peppers. Blend well and set aside.

Clean the mushrooms and remove the stems. Brush the outsides and shells with olive oil, and sprinkle about 2 tbsp of the balsamic vinegar over the cavity of each. Place on a greased baking pan, gill side up. Divide the bread crumb mixture evenly on top of the mushroom cavities. Sprinkle the remaining Parmesan cheese evenly on top.

Bake for 10 to 12 minutes or until warmed and slightly softened. Cut each mushroom into 4 triangles, or leave whole, and place on 4 salad plates. Serve with a knife and fork.

PREPARATION TIME: 15 minutes

DIANE'S SECRETS

For a variation, after heating the mushrooms, top each cavity with thin slices of mozzarella. Brush with a little pesto and top with roasted chopped garlic and strips of roasted peppers.

EILEEN DWILLIE'S OLIVE TAPENADE

MAKES ABOUT 1 CUP

Eileen Dwillie's tapenade is the best! It goes great with my Pita Triangles (page 119) and Bagel Crisps (page 124).

INGREDIENTS
1 cup black niçoise olives, pitted
4 cloves garlic, peeled
4 anchovy fillets (optional)
2 tbsp drained capers (optional)
Juice of ½ lemon
½ cup olive oil
Pepper to taste

METHOD
Put the olives, garlic, anchovies, capers and lemon juice in a food processor. Pulse to mix. With the machine running, slowly add the olive oil until the mixture forms a medium to fine purée. Season with pepper. (Can be stored, covered, in the fridge for up to 5 days.)

PREPARATION TIME: 10 minutes

DIANE'S SECRETS

Most delis carry niçoise olives. If you can't find them, use another good variety of olives in brine, such as the Greek calamata variety. Most tapenades include anchovies and capers, but if you don't enjoy them, they can be left out.

My longtime friend, Eileen Dwillies, has been teaching cooking almost as long as I have. We both share a passion for exploring the foods of the world. Eileen became a superb food stylist and had her own television cooking show. One of her dreams was to open her own cooking school in France, which she eventually did.

In 1992, my twin brother David, and his wife Dianne, joined Doug and me at Eileen and husband Paul's retreat in Curnier, in southern France, near Provence. We spent a relaxing week surrounded by olive groves and lavender fields and visiting the local farmers' markets, wineries and bistros. We vowed then that we would return to Provence, and in the summer of 1999 we did just that, once again to be treated to the splendour and wonderful foods of that beautiful region. 🚲

CAREN McSHERRY VALAGAO'S SANTA FE CHICKEN WITH TORTILLA CHIPS

SERVES 6

Caren McSherry Valagao is one of Vancouver's most passionate and creative chefs. Caren has her own always-sold-out cooking school, as well as a gourmet kitchen boutique located at her husband's José's business, Continental Importers, which is the premier supplier of specialty food products for restaurants throughout British Columbia. Together, Caren and José share a passion for the best in food and wines.

Caren is also a cookbook author and a radio and television personality. She and I have worked on many fundraising projects for the Les Dames d'Escoffier organization, and we share billing on the BCTV's *Saturday Chef* series, along with Nathan Fong. José was a wonderful mentor to me when we opened our Tomato Café in 1991. Caren and José are very special friends and colleagues.

Caren describes her Santa Fe Chicken as "a colourful, flavourful dish that can be served as an appetizer or as a main course with steaming rice. I particularly like it with blue corn chips. Just dig in, but beware – it's very hard to stop!"

INGREDIENTS
½ cup olive oil, divided
1 yellow onion, diced (about 1 cup)
4 garlic cloves, minced
2 red peppers, seeded and diced
1 can (14 oz) kernel corn, drained
3 boneless chicken breasts, skinned and cut into
   bite-size pieces
2 to 3 tbsp chili powder
1 tsp ground cumin
½ bunch cilantro, chopped
1 tsp crushed, dried red-pepper flakes (optional)
Salt to taste
Warm flour tortillas or corn chips

METHOD

Heat ¼ cup of the oil in a large fry pan. When the oil is hot, add the onion and 2 of the garlic cloves. Cook for about 5 minutes, or until softened. Add the red peppers and corn and cook over medium heat for about 5 minutes more, or until vegetables are soft. Remove and set aside.

In the same pan, heat the remaining ¼ cup oil. When the oil is hot, add the 2 remaining garlic cloves along with the chicken. Cook, turning occasionally, for about 10 minutes or until well browned. Stir in the chili, cumin, cilantro and red pepper flakes. Add the reserved corn mixture and heat through to blend the flavours. Taste and season with salt. Serve on a decorative platter garnished with wedges of warm flour tortillas or corn chips with your choice of Mexican beer.

PREPARATION TIME: 35 minutes

FIRE AND ICE FRUIT SALSA

I call this salsa my "teaser" with flavours to test your tastebuds! Fabulous with crab cakes and grilled tuna, it's best made the day ahead or early on the day of serving.

INGREDIENTS
1 cup fresh or canned pineapple, chopped
1 cup fresh or canned mango, chopped
¼ cup red onion, finely chopped
3 jalapeno peppers seeded and finely chopped
    (about ⅓ cup)
Zest and juice of 2 limes
½ cup cilantro, chopped
3 tbsp fresh mint, chopped
1 red pepper, finely chopped
1 tbsp honey
2 tbsp raspberry or white wine vinegar

METHOD
In a bowl, combine all ingredients and refrigerate. Bring to room temperature before serving.

PREPARATION TIME: 15 minutes

AIOLI

Easy to make and great with pommes frites or grilled vegetables.

INGREDIENTS
2 cloves garlic, peeled and finely chopped
½ tsp salt
2 large egg yolks
Juice of ½ lemon (optional)
Pepper to taste
1 cup olive oil

METHOD
In a bowl, combine the garlic and salt, pressing down with the back of a spoon to form a paste. (A mortar and pestle works well.) Add the egg yolks, one at a time, lemon juice and pepper; blend well. Add the olive oil, a few teaspoons at a time, whisking continually until the mixture is thickened. Refrigerate.

PREPARATION TIME: 5 minutes

DIANE'S SECRETS

If the aioli separates, slowly whisk in half an egg yolk to bring it back to consistency of mayonnaise.
Keep it for 2 days only in the refrigerator, as the garlic takes on a slightly bitter taste after that. The lemon juice is optional, but I like the citrus complement.
For Red Pepper Aioli, leave out the lemon juice and add 1 cup roasted, chopped red pepper before you add the olive oil.

OCEAN POINTE RESORT DUCK SALAD WITH CRISPY WONTONS

SERVES 6

In 1994, when Doug and I acted as honourary mayors of the international athletes' village for the Commonwealth Games in Victoria, we joined our friends John and Lynne Landy at Ocean Pointe Resort Hotel. We loved the food and the ambiance at Ocean Pointe, so much so that we returned in 1998 to spend the weekend and to enjoy dinner in their restaurant. We were pampered by executive chef Craig Stoneman and sous chef Neil Antolin. Their Duck Salad was outstanding. This is an adaptation of their recipe, which I featured on one of my BCTV *Saturday Chefs* series, hosted by the dynamic Jill Krop. The wontons are optional but are an added treat to this tangy Asian salad.

There was no excuse in the nineties for not making a sensational salad. The markets were full of every type of green, vegetable and fruit imaginable. Dressings ranged from the basic Caesar, Italian or balsamic vinaigrettes, to mixtures with herbed-infused oils and vinegars, fruit purées and exotic spices. Low-fat combinations with intense flavour were the most requested. Here are a few of my favourite greens and toppings from the nineties. ❧

INGREDIENTS

SALAD

3 duck breasts, marinated
3 bunches of spinach, cleaned,
    broken in half if large
1 whole radicchio, sliced into thin strips (chiffonade)
30 enoki mushrooms
    (5 per person) (optional)
18 peeled slices of oranges, grilled, if desired
Black or white toasted sesame seeds,
    or a combination

MARINADE

2 tsp pure sesame oil
2 tsp Chinese chili paste
3 tbsp soy sauce
2 tbsp green peppercorns, crushed
2 tbsp fresh peeled ginger, grated
1 tsp garlic, chopped
3 tbsp orange juice concentrate
2 tbsp pure apple juice

METHOD

Combine all marinade ingredients and marinate the duck breasts for 12 to 24 hours. Drain off the liquid.

Prepare the vinaigrette (see below) and refrigerate until ready to serve.

Bake the breasts in the oven at 350°F for 8 to 10 minutes or until medium rare. Slice the breasts very thin on an angle and refrigerate while preparing the greens.

Toss the spinach and radicchio with enough dressing to coat. Add the mushrooms and the duck slices. On each salad plate, place the orange slices on the bottom of the plate, 3 per person. Place the salad greens on top of the oranges, exposing the oranges a little. Garnish with the sesame seeds on top and the vinaigrette around the outside of the salad plates. Serve immediately, with Crispy Wontons if desired (see below).

SOYA GINGER VINAIGRETTE

Blend together, 1¼ cup vegetable oil, ½ cup soy sauce, ½ cup rice wine vinegar, ⅓ cup brown sugar, 1 tbsp chopped shallots, 2 tbsp grated fresh ginger and 2 tsp pure sesame oil. Refrigerate. (Can be made a day or two ahead of using.)

CRISPY WONTONS

Cut 1 lb wonton skins into thin strips or wedges. Cover the base of a large fry pan with about 1 inch peanut oil; heat. (Peanut oil is best for deep frying as it does not smoke at high temperatures.) The oil is hot enough when a strip of wonton skin begins to curl. Add strips a few at a time and deep fry for a few seconds or until they turn golden. Remove with a strainer spoon and drain well on paper towels. Put into a serving basket and set aside. The crispy wontons should not be cooked until the day of serving.

PREPARATION TIME: 45 minutes

DIANE'S SECRETS

Green peppercorns are found in specialty food sections of food stores. They are packed in brine and have a unique fruity taste. Try them in sauces for meats and poultry for an interesting taste!

In 1954 Doug had competed in what was then called the British Empire Games, held in Vancouver, where he received a silver medal in the men's 4x100 relay. During those Games, Doug met John Landy and Roger Bannister, the first two athletes to break the four-minute mile barrier. Many Vancouverites remember those Games when Bannister narrowly defeated Landy in the famous mile race. In Victoria in 1994, Doug and I were thrilled to host John Landy and his wife Lynne, and Sir Roger and Lady Bannister. It was fun to relive the memories of former Games with them.

ITALIAN ROASTED VEGETABLE TOMATO SALAD

SERVES 6

In 1996, Doug and I joined Umberto Menghi as hosts at his glorious Villa Delia in Tuscany, near Pisa. It was 10 days of the best cooking classes and the most delectable food and wine we've ever enjoyed! Sixteen others from Vancouver, Toronto, Los Angeles and Sun Valley were part of our energetic, fun-loving group.

My brother David and his wife Dianne joined us, as well, to celebrate David's and my 60th birthday while in Tuscany. Our role, as hosts with Umberto, was to add a "lifestyle" component to the cooking classes. Each morning Doug and I would lead the most enthusiastic early risers in a power walk. At nine o'clock our cooking classes began. But first we were served a continental breakfast with the Villa's scrumptious fig tarts, Italian breads and homemade jams.

Umberto's sister, Marietta, taught us Italian classics of her family that had been handed down for centuries. Umberto would do the translating, as we all frantically wrote down the ▶

This recipe, which I developed, brings back so many special moments at Umberto Menghi's Villa Delia, with his sister Marietta and her husband Silvano, and the fabulous Italian meals we enjoyed there in 1996. I love serving this roasted vegetable salad for a family picnic or barbecue. It makes lots, but it's the only salad you need. It takes a little time to make, but most of it can be done in advance and it's well worth the effort.

INGREDIENTS
4 cups large croutons
Olive oil
4 sweet peppers (2 red, 1 yellow, 1 orange), cut into
    2-inch squares
1 red onion, sliced in small chunks
1 fennel bulb, sliced in small chunks (reserve a few
    chopped leaves to toss with the salad)
2 zucchini (1 yellow, 1 green), sliced ½-inch thick
2 Japanese eggplant, sliced ½-inch thick
Salt and pepper to taste
½ cup calamata olives, pitted
3 medium red tomatoes, chopped
3 yellow tomatoes, chopped
½ cup grated Parmesan cheese
2 cups mixed greens, or arugula

METHOD

Prepare dressing (see below) and set aside.

Prepare croutons by cutting bread in ½-inch pieces. Toss with olive oil to coat, and bake in a 350°F oven for 25 to 30 minutes or until golden and crispy. (Can be made up to a week ahead and stored in a sealed container.)

Oil 2 cookie sheets. In a bowl, toss peppers, onion and fennel with enough olive oil to coat; spread on a cookie sheet. In another bowl, do the same with the zucchini and eggplant and spread on the other cookie sheet. Roast in oven at 400°F for 20 to 30 minutes or until *al dente*. Sprinkle with a little salt and pepper. (Vegetables can be roasted several hours before serving, covered with plastic wrap and refrigerated.)

To serve, in a large salad bowl toss roasted vegetables with remaining ingredients except the mixed greens. Add enough dressing to coat. Let sit about 15 minutes. Add the greens, reserved fennel leaves, and more pepper to taste. Pass remaining dressing if needed. Serve immediately, as the croutons will go soggy!

DRESSING

In a bowl, whisk together ¼ cup pesto (your own, or from a deli), 1 tbsp Dijon mustard, ¼ cup balsamic vinegar, ¼ cup chopped fresh basil and pepper to taste. Add 1½ cups olive oil very slowly and whisk until smooth. Can be made a few days ahead; will keep up to a week in the refrigerator.

PREPARATION TIME: 20 minutes

ingredients in the little notebooks he provided. On the first day of classes, Umberto exclaimed, "The best way to learn a recipe is to observe, and then to write it down in your own words." And he was right.

When we returned home and attempted to recreate the recipes, I would compare my recipe book to Doug's. His was so neat, while my recipes were scrawled all over the pages. Between the two books, fortunately, I was able to make sense of the ingredients. Then all Marietta's cooking techniques came back to me!

Besides being a great translator, Umberto is a wonderful host. We were totally pampered at his Villa. We visited wine museums in Sienna, dined at superb restaurants, relaxed at an amazing health spa and hiked seaside villages. But we all agreed that the best was the Villa itself, sitting down every evening to at least a six-course meal, with the Villa's fine wines. Laughter and conversation surrounded us all — it was magic! ♣

THE WEST COASTER SALMON SALAD

This unique salad has become a signature dish at the Tomato. On our menu the description reads: "A warm salad: B.C. Indian-candy smoked salmon with warm maple-balsamic vinaigrette on a bed of spring mixed greens, topped with chèvre." How much better can it get? I love the marriage of the sweet-sour taste of the vinaigrette with the hint of pure maple syrup and balsamic vinegar.

INGREDIENTS
½ lb peppered Indian candy smoked salmon strips (such as Westcoast Select)
6 cups mixed greens
½ red pepper, sliced into thin julienne strips
½ yellow pepper, sliced into thin julienne strips
8 oz crumbled chèvre

METHOD
Prepare the Maple Balsamic Vinaigrette (see below) and set aside.

Just before serving, peel the skin off the salmon, slice diagonally into ¼-inch thick slices. Set aside. Divide the greens evenly among 6 salad plates, mounding them high.

Heat the vinaigrette in a skillet over low heat. Add the slices of salmon and the peppers. Heat briefly to warm. On each salad plate, divide the salmon, peppers and dressing mixture equally over the greens. Top with a good sprinkling of chèvre. Serve immediately.

MAPLE BALSAMIC VINAIGRETTE
Whisk together 5 tbsp balsamic vinegar (or to taste), 1 tsp Dijon mustard, 3 tbsp pure maple syrup and pepper to taste. Add 1 cup light olive oil (or a blend of vegetable and olive oils) very slowly and whisk until smooth. Taste for the right balance of vinegar and maple syrup, adding more of either if necessary. (Can be made up to 3 days ahead and refrigerated.)

PREPARATION TIME: 20 minutes

The Commonwealth Games, held in Victoria in 1994, were one of the most successful in the history of the Games. Victoria went all out to host "The Friendly Games," with over 15,000 volunteers contributing their time. Doug and I took part as the honourary mayors of the International Athletes Village at the University of Victoria. It was our responsibility to greet the athletes and officials at 63 flag-raising ceremonies, and to host royalty, heads of state and team leaders.

CHILLED GEORGIA PEACH-MANGO SOUP

Serves 6 to 8

During the extremely hot summer days in Atlanta during the 1996 Olympic Games, everyone was looking to cool down by eating and drinking anything cold. As soon as we arrived at the Olympic stadium each day, we would purchase 2 frozen lemon popsicles, which would satisfy us for the first 20 minutes!

Atlanta had many outstanding restaurants. They usually had cold peach soup on their menu because the peaches were then at their peak. One of my favourites combined peaches with mangoes.

So, in tribute to all those tasty Georgian peaches, this is my version of their soup.

INGREDIENTS
12 fresh peaches, peeled, seeded and sliced
3 fresh mangoes, peeled, seeded and sliced
Juice of 2 limes
¼ to ½ cup fresh orange juice
¼ cup sparkling white wine, peach schnapps or peach juice
¾ cup sour cream
3 tbsp peach schnapps or orange juice
2 peaches, peeled, seeded and chopped finely
Few sprigs fresh mint

METHOD
Several hours before serving, in a food processor blend the 12 peaches and the mangoes with the lime juice. Add enough orange juice to thin slightly. Add the wine. Chill in the refrigerator.

In a small bowl, blend the sour cream with the peach schnapps. Refrigerate.

To serve, divide the peach-mango mixture evenly among 6 to 8 small bowls. Swirl the sour cream mixture over top. Sprinkle with a few chopped peaches and top with a sprig of mint.

PREPARATION TIME: 10 minutes

Atlanta has at least 35 different "Peachtree" street names in honour of their famous peaches. During the 1996 Olympic Games in Atlanta, we taxed our nerves trying to decipher which Peachtree cutoff to take, while driving into the city with thousands of other Olympic tourists. However, with Charmaine Crook's husband Anders as our navigator, we never missed a race for going the wrong way! And because downtown parking was easy to find (Georgians were asked not to drive downtown during the Games), we forgave the town planners for all those Peachtrees! &

KASEY WILSON'S ROASTED RED PEPPER SOUP WITH SAMBUCA

SERVES 6

In 1996–97, I was president of the Vancouver chapter of Les Dames d'Escoffier, and also chairperson, along with Caren McSherry Valagao, of our spring fundraiser event. We decided to present a culinary celebration to be held at Vancouver's Delta Place, which is now the Metropolitan Hotel. Our goal was to establish a scholarship fund for women wishing to enter or further their career in the culinary and hospitality professions. The five chefs from Les Dames d'Escoffier who participated in the fundraiser and presented the evening menu were Margaret Chisholm, Kasey Wilson, Lesley Stowe, Caren McSherry Valagao and me. The rest of our Les Dames membership made up our kitchen team, servers and hosts. Our dishes received rave reviews that evening from our guests. Kasey Wilson has had to step down from our association since then, but her Roasted Red-Pepper Soup with Sambuca was a big hit that evening!

INGREDIENTS
¼ cup butter
3 large onions, sliced
2 large cloves garlic
1 tsp salt
4 cups roasted sweet red peppers (available in jars, or roast your own)
3 cups chicken stock
½ cup whipping cream
Salt and pepper to taste
Pinch cayenne pepper (or to taste)
1 red pepper
Sambuca

METHOD

Melt the butter in a large, heavy saucepan over medium heat. Add the onions, garlic and salt, and sauté for 10 minutes or until tender. Add the roasted peppers and chicken stock; simmer for 15 minutes. Pour the mixture into a food processor or blender and purée until smooth. Transfer the purée to a saucepan and bring to a boil. Stir in the whipping cream. Season with salt, pepper and cayenne. Thin with additional chicken broth if necessary.

Serve the soup in individual bowls. Cut the red pepper into 6 small wedges, carving out a little circle in the middle to hold the sambuca. Save some pepper to chop finely for garnish. Fill the pepper wedges with sambuca and float on the soup. Sprinkle the remaining chopped peppers over top. Light the sambuca in the wedges at the table just before calling the guests to dinner.

PREPARATION TIME: 30 minutes

DIANE'S SECRETS *Remove all the charred skin remaining on the roasted peppers before adding to the onion and garlic mixture; otherwise you'll have a red soup speckled with black!*

Les Dames d'Escoffier is an association of leading women in the fields of food, beverage and hospitality. Their original charter was granted by the mostly male members of Les Amis d'Escoffier in New York in 1976. Julia Child is a member and so was writer M.F.K. Fisher. In 1992, the British Columbia chapter was founded, the first outside the United States. Now, Australia has joined the international association.

The Vancouver chapter of Les Dames started with 26 founding members, and in 1999 we had 40. Our mission is to enhance the image of women working in the food, wine and hospitality industries by recognizing their achievements, giving them a worldwide networking system and encouraging involvement in community service programs. It has been one of the most rewarding organizations I have been involved in. The enthusiasm, expertise and dedication of our members is incredible. I am proud to be a part of this dynamic group. ✍

ROASTED SQUASH SOUP WITH PUMPKIN SEEDS

Whenever Doug and I are in New York, we dine at Matthew Kenney's various restaurants. At the first one he ever opened, Matthew's, he serves a divine squash soup, and this is my adaptation of it. In this recipe, which is surprisingly quick to make, Moroccan spices reign supreme. In 1999 it was the hit of my cooking class at Gail Norton's popular The Cookbook Co. Cooks cooking school and specialty food and wine store. Butternut squash is the perfect fall/winter soup ingredient, and Thanksgiving dinner is a perfect time for trying it out. Best of all, it's low in fat! Serve small portions, as it is very filling.

Whoever tires of homemade soups? Often, soup can be a meal in itself, served with lots of hearty bread and a side salad. At our Tomato Café, from the moment we opened our doors in 1991 we've been known for our soups. Customers come from all over Vancouver, some even driving an hour from the North Shore, just for a bowl of our hearty, made-from-scratch soups! Here are some of my most-loved soups of the nineties. ✑

INGREDIENTS
3 lbs butternut squash, peeled and cut into
   ¾-inch cubes (about 8 cups)
2 tbsp olive oil
¾ tsp ground cinnamon
¼ tsp ground cloves
¾ tsp ground ginger
¾ tsp Madras curry powder
10 cups chicken stock
1 cup plain yogurt, at room temperature
Salt and pepper to taste
Pumpkin seed oil, or plain yogurt
1 cup roasted pumpkin seeds
   (see Diane's secrets, page 91)

METHOD

Preheat the oven to 400°F. In a large bowl toss the squash with just enough olive oil to coat. Add the cinnamon, cloves, ginger and curry powder; toss well. Spread the spiced squash cubes in a single layer on a large cookie sheet. Bake, covered with foil, for 10 minutes; remove the foil and continue to roast for another 10 to 15 minutes until softened. Set aside.

In a large pot, bring the chicken stock to a boil. Add the roasted squash cubes. Bring to a boil, reduce the heat, and simmer for 10 minutes. Cool, then purée in a food processor until very smooth. Mix about ½ cup of the soup with the yogurt, then add the yogurt to the pot of soup. Add salt and pepper to taste. (Can be made up to this point and refrigerated for a day or two before serving.)

To serve, reheat until hot. If too thick, add a little more chicken stock. Pour into the soup bowls and drizzle with about 1 tsp pumpkin seed oil and a few roasted pumpkin seeds.

PREPARATION TIME: 40 minutes

JACQUES AND SIEGFRIED'S PROVENÇAL ZUCCHINI SOUP

SERVES 4 TO 6

In the summer of 1999, Doug and I spent seven weeks in Provence and our family joined us during their travels in France. One Sunday, our daughter Jennifer and her partner Vincent, along with our niece Diana and her husband Doug, joined us for lunch at a quaint restaurant, La Pause, in the hilltop village of Gordes. Much to our delight, we discovered that the owners were a French Canadian, Jacques Friscourt, and his partner Siegfried Huck. We found out that whenever the Queen Mother visited her English friends in Gordes, Jacques would cook for her. They gave us the royal treatment too! We had a memorable afternoon in their restaurant, which they had converted from a small house in the heart of this magnificent village. Later, Jacques sent me his specialty soup recipe along with its history. As he describes it: "This soup was La Venus de Gordes favourite dish, mostly because her husband did not like it – and she didn't like him! With the help of her lover she chopped off her husband's head and threw it in the well of her courtyard. Then she and her lover ran off to French Guyana! All that in the 19th century!" Bon appetit!

INGREDIENTS
3 tbsp olive oil
1 large onion, peeled and chopped
2 large cloves garlic, peeled and chopped
6 cups chicken stock
4 medium zucchini, chopped
3 medium potatoes, peeled and chopped
1 small bunch basil, stems removed and
    chopped (about ¼ cup)
Salt and pepper to taste
Whipping cream or plain yogurt
Additional fresh basil, julienne strips

METHOD

In a large pot, heat the oil and sauté the onions and garlic until softened. Add the chicken stock, zucchini, potatoes, basil, salt and pepper. Bring to a boil; cover and cook 45 minutes. Cool. Purée in a food processor or blender. (Can be made ahead to this point and refrigerated.)

To serve, reheat the soup until hot, pour into bowls and drizzle a little whipping cream on top. Garnish with a few strips of fresh basil.

PREPARATION TIME: 50 minutes.

 DIANE'S SECRETS   *Best made a day ahead. When reheating, if soup seems too thick, add a little more chicken stock.*

ORZO

SERVES 8

Orzo is a rice-shaped pasta which can usually be obtained from Italian or specialty markets. It's a perfect accompaniment to chicken or to Villa Delia's Melanzane-Riepieni (page 195).

Less fat: Eliminate butter; just add a little more stock.

INGREDIENTS
2 cups raw orzo
4 to 6 tbsp butter
4 to 6 tbsp chicken or vegetable stock
6 to 8 tbsp Parmesan cheese, freshly grated
Salt and pepper to taste
4 to 5 tbsp parsley, finely chopped

METHOD
Cook the orzo in a large Dutch oven with plenty of salted water for 10 to 12 minutes or until just barely tender and doubled in volume. Do not overcook. Drain well in a colander, rinsing with plenty of cold water to remove excess starch. Drain again. (Can be made ahead and stored in covered bowl in the refrigerator.)

Melt the butter in a large, heavy fry pan; add the orzo and heat through. Add just enough stock to moisten the orzo; stir in the Parmesan cheese. Add the salt and pepper to taste. Toss with chopped parsley and serve.

If made ahead, before serving reheat until hot, adding more stock and cheese if necessary to keep it moist.

PREPARATION TIME: 20 minutes

DIANE'S SECRETS
Try adding sautéed mushrooms, prosciutto and roasted peppers for a whole meal in itself. For a nippier pasta, add more Parmesan cheese.

VILLA DELIA'S MELANZANE-RIEPIENI (STUFFED EGGPLANT)

SERVES 4

When Doug and I were at Umberto Menghi's Villa Delia in Tuscany in 1996, every meal was a masterpiece. The produce was fresh from the garden, the seafood, meats and poultry rushed to the villa every morning from the suppliers, and the baking was just out of the oven every day! And did we eat! Italians enjoy long, leisurely meals, savouring every bite. Our group adapted to this relaxed pace of dining, and as a result, we left the dining room feeling very content, but never overfull.

This dish was voted one of the best at Villa Delia. The combination of proscuitto and Emmantaler cheese rolled in eggplant is a meal in itself when served with orzo (page 194) or as an appetizer.

INGREDIENTS
1 large eggplant, unpeeled, sliced very thin
   lengthwise (about 10 slices)
Salt
2 cups fine, dry bread crumbs
Olive or sunflower oil, or a blend of both
10 thin slices proscuitto or ham
10 thin slices Emmantaler cheese
2 cups tomato sauce
½ to ¾ cups Parmesan cheese

METHOD
Sprinkle the eggplant with salt and let sit for about 30 minutes. Rinse the eggplant and pat well to dry. Pat both sides with the bread crumbs. Heat a little oil in a fry pan, and sauté the eggplant slices on both sides until golden. Don't crowd the eggplant; do the slices in batches. Pat dry with paper towels. On each slice of eggplant, place a slice of proscuitto, then a slice of cheese. Roll up, jelly roll fashion. Place in a 13x9x2-inch casserole. Pour the tomato sauce over top to cover evenly; sprinkle Parmesan cheese over all. (Can be made ahead of time up to this point and kept in the refrigerator for a day.) Bake at 350°F for 25 to 30 minutes or until hot.

PREPARATION TIME: 40 minutes

DIANE'S SECRETS

This dish can be served hot or cold, but I prefer it served warm with a side dish of pasta.

ROASTED GARLIC POTATOES AND ROOT VEGETABLES

SERVES AS MANY AS DESIRED;
ALLOW 1 PIECE OF EACH VEGETABLE PER PERSON.

In the nineties, anything roasted was a big hit. It can complement a main course, or be served just on its own.

INGREDIENTS
A combination of these or other vegetables (use your imagination!): new baby potatoes, parsnips, turnips, beets, carrots and garlic cloves.
Olive oil
Fresh rosemary sprigs, finely chopped, or herbes de Provence (see Diane's secrets)
Salt and pepper

METHOD
Peel all vegetables except the new potatoes. In a large bowl, combine the olive oil with the herbs, salt and pepper. (For each cup of olive oil, add 4 tbsp chopped fresh rosemary, or 2 tbsp dried herbes de Provence; salt and pepper to taste.) Toss the vegetables separately in the olive oil mixture, just enough to coat. Place on oiled cookie sheets, spreading them out. Do not overcrowd vegetables.

Roast uncovered at 350°F for 25 minutes. Toss and brush with a little more of the herbed oil if needed. Continue to roast for another 25 minutes longer or until the vegetables are cooked.

Serve immediately. (If prepared ahead, reheat in a 350°F oven, uncovered, 25 minutes or until warmed.)

PREPARATION TIME: 40 minutes

DIANE'S SECRETS

Herbes de Provence is an herb mixture used in many French dishes. It is an equal blend of dried oregano, thyme, marjoram and savory. You can find it in specialty food shops. Try these vegetables with Aioli (page 181) as a dipping sauce.

STUFFED TOMATOES À LA PROVENÇALE

SERVES 6

When we were growing up, Mom would serve stuffed tomatoes with macaroni and cheese or the Sunday roast. In the nineties, we put a fancy French name to this old classic and it became très chic! Whatever you call these tomatoes, they are delicious and go beautifully with the Mushroom Cheese Strata (page 32).

INGREDIENTS

3 large tomatoes, cut in half crosswise
1 cup soft bread crumbs
¼ cup Parmesan cheese, grated
1 large clove garlic, crushed (optional)
1 tbsp fresh basil, finely chopped, or ½ tsp herbes
   de Provence (see Diane's secrets, page 196)
Salt and pepper to taste
3 tbsp olive oil

METHOD

With your fingers, remove the excess seeds from the tomatoes, keeping the tomatoes intact. To prevent the tomatoes from becoming too soggy when baking, turn them upside down on paper towels for a few minutes to drain off the excess juices. Pat dry.

Blend together remaining ingredients. Place tomatoes in a lightly oiled casserole; don't overcrowd. Top each tomato half with an equal portion of the bread mixture, pressing down slightly. Sprinkle a little more Parmesan cheese on top of each tomato.

Bake at 350°F for 25 minutes or until the tomatoes are warm and the topping is golden.

PREPARATION TIME: 10 minutes

KAREN BARNABY'S SPAGHETTI SQUASH WITH ROASTED GARLIC AND SUN-DRIED TOMATOES

SERVES 4 TO 6

Karen Barnaby is the executive chef of one of the top seafood restaurants in Canada, The Fish House, in Vancouver's Stanley Park. Her two cookbooks, *Pacific Passions* and *Screamingly Good Food*, are Canadian best-sellers, and she was instrumental in coordinating the highly acclaimed cookbook *The Girls Who Dish*, published in 1998, and its sequel, *The Girls Who Dish: Seconds, Anyone?* Karen is one of the most dedicated members of our Les Dames d'Escoffier organization, and she spearheads our scholarship committee. What I most admire about Karen is her super talent as a chef, her fabulous sense of humour, and her constant, cheerful laugh. She's a total winner, and her Spaghetti Squash is fabulous. Her comments on the recipe: "For some, sun-dried tomatoes and roasted garlic have had their 15 minutes of fame. However, they have become firmly entrenched in our cooking vocabulary and here they work wonders with the flavour and texture of spaghetti squash."

INGREDIENTS

1 small spaghetti squash, about 2 lb
½ cup water
1½ tbsp cider vinegar
½ tsp salt
¼ tsp ground black pepper
3 sun-dried tomatoes, rehydrated or packed in oil
10 cloves roasted garlic (see Diane's secrets)
½ cup extra-virgin olive oil
2 medium ripe tomatoes, seeded and diced into
    ¼-inch pieces
½ cup parsley, chopped
¼ cup basil leaves, torn into small pieces

METHOD

Preheat the oven to 350°F. Cut the squash in half lengthwise, and place cut side down in a baking dish. Pour the water around the squash and cover tightly with tin foil or a lid. Bake for 1 hour or until tender. While the squash is baking, prepare the rest of the ingredients.

In a food processor or blender, purée vinegar, salt, pepper, sun-dried tomatoes and garlic. With the motor on, add the olive oil in a slow steady stream. Set aside.

Scrape the cooked squash out of the shell into a bowl. Toss with the olive oil mixture. To serve hot, combine with tomatoes, parsley and basil and serve immediately. To serve cold, let cool to room temperature before tossing with the remaining ingredients.

PREPARATION TIME: 1½ hours

DIANE'S SECRETS

To roast garlic, heat oven to 400°F. Take 1 whole head of garlic and remove as much of the loose skin as you can. Slice across the top, about ⅛-inch deep. Rub in a little olive oil to moisten, then wrap in a piece of aluminum foil. Put in a small ovenproof dish and roast for 30 to 40 minutes or until the garlic is soft and tender, checking frequently after 25 minutes. Cool, then squeeze out the garlic needed for the recipe.

ALLAN'S BRIE AND STRAWBERRY
FRENCH TOAST

SERVES 4

One of our first chefs at the Tomato Café, Allan Morgan, served his Brie and Straw-berry French Toast during special Sunday Brunches. Allan is not only a talented chef, he has received many accolades for acting on the stage, television and in movies. He also has a great singing voice, and some of my favourite memories are of the times Allan and I sang together in our wild Tomato kitchen. I've always had a desire to be a singer, but alas, with a voice like mine, there's no hope. But at the Tomato, my staff had no ▶

Whenever this specialty of Chef Allan Morgan appeared on our weekend brunch menu at the Tomato Café, it sold out in no time. Customers would phone weeks ahead to ask when it would next be served.

I enjoy Sunday brunch for a change, rather than having the family over for dinner. It's leisurely, casual, and it gives you the chance to try out some egg dishes. Sometimes I'll make a frittata or omelette, sometimes this French toast favourite. A platter of fresh fruit, scones or toast, fresh juices and coffee round out this noon affair!

INGREDIENTS
⅔ cup whole milk
5 large eggs, beaten
1 tsp vanilla
¼ tsp cinnamon
Pinch nutmeg
3 to 4 tsp granulated sugar
8 slices (1½ inch) day-old sourdough
    or French bread
24 slices (¼ inch) brie
24 fresh strawberries, thinly sliced
2 to 4 tbsp butter
Icing sugar
Maple syrup

METHOD

Whisk together the milk, eggs, vanilla, cinnamon, nutmeg and sugar, blending well. Set aside.

Cut through each slice of bread horizontally to form a pocket. Avoid slicing the bread all the way through on both sides. Place 3 slices of brie in pocket, then top with a layer of strawberries. Press down lightly. (Pockets can be prepared a few hours in advance and covered with plastic wrap.) Refrigerate.

Soak each bread slice in the egg mixture, coating well on both sides. Set aside and refrigerate for about 15 minutes, covered. Melt butter in a fry pan and sauté the stuffed bread over medium heat until golden, then flip over and cook the other side. (You may have to sauté bread in 2 batches unless you have a very large fry pan.) Serve immediately, or keep warm in the oven at a low temperature.

Sprinkle with icing sugar. Serve with maple syrup and additional sliced strawberries. Also good with a strawberry purée.

PREPARATION TIME: 40 minutes

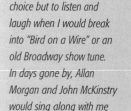

choice but to listen and laugh when I would break into "Bird on a Wire" or an old Broadway show tune. In days gone by, Allan Morgan and John McKinstry would sing along with me as the lunch crowd peered into the kitchen to see if we'd gone totally mad. Then the waiters would join in, and sometimes the customers would pick up a line or two. Other times Bonnie Panych would start the staff lattes going as we broke into "It's Caffe Latte Time," while dancing the cancan. Those were the days! &

DIANE'S SECRETS

Try dipping both sides of the French toast in finely crushed corn flake crumbs just before you put them in the fry pan. C'est si bon! James Beard introduced French toast rolled in corn flake crumbs for the breakfast menu of the Santa Fe Railroads in the early sixties. The Holland America Line features it on their cruise ships in the nineties!

JAZZY GARY'S TARRAGON CHICKEN AVOCADO SANDWICH

MAKES 6 SANDWICHES

Chef Gary Thompson, who plays a mean saxophone, came to the Tomato Café from Toronto in the early nineties, after a successful run with his own café. He has now moved on to the world of computers, and has established a "private chef" business in Vancouver.

INGREDIENTS
6 boneless, skinless chicken breasts, cooked and
    diced into ½-inch cubes
3 sticks of celery, chopped
6 to 7 green onions, chopped
1 large red pepper, cut into small squares
¾ cup mayonnaise
½ cup fresh tarragon, or 1 tbsp dried
Salt and pepper to taste
1 head of romaine lettuce, shredded
12 slices of whole wheat or French bread
3 avocados, seeded, peeled, cut in half, and sliced

METHOD
Combine the chicken, celery, onions, pepper, mayonnaise, tarragon, salt and pepper. Divide the lettuce among the 6 sandwiches. Top with the chicken mixture and layer the avocado on each sandwich.

PREPARATION TIME: 15 minutes

DIANE'S SECRETS

I like this chicken salad sandwich with chopped fresh basil as a substitute for the tarragon. The chicken mixture is also great as a salad on a bed of the romaine, garnished with the avocado slices.

VICKI'S FRENCH MACARONI GRATIN

SERVES 4

Macaroni and cheese in Paris? When we saw this on the menu in a Left Bank bistro in 1992, we just had to order it. It added a French twist to the North American classic, and it was great! Of course, we ordered a robust French red wine and lots of their famous bread to round out our meal. I dedicate this recipe to Vicki Gabereau, with whom I've shared so many great cooking experiences. This one's officially yours, Vicki! Enjoy!

INGREDIENTS
4 cups short tubular pasta, such as small, thin penne
½ cup niçoise black olives, pitted and chopped (or any brine-cured imported black olives)
5 tomatoes, peeled, seeded and coarsely chopped
1 tbsp fresh thyme, chopped finely
2 tbsp olive oil
Salt and pepper to taste
1½ cups chèvre cheese, crumbled
1 cup Parmesan cheese, grated

METHOD
Cook the pasta according to the directions on package. Drain. Add all remaining ingredients except the Parmesan cheese. Spoon into a 13x9x2-inch casserole. Sprinkle Parmesan cheese evenly over top. Bake at 400°F 25 to 30 minutes or until hot. Pass more Parmesan cheese at the table.

PREPARATION TIME: 15 minutes

I have enjoyed cooking with Vicki Gabereau on several occasions. When she had her popular CBC radio show, it was always a challenge to make the recipes "sound delicious" on air! On one show I prepared crème brûlée. As we tasted this rich dessert, Vicki exclaimed, "Mmmmmm, this is so good! Wow! It's so creamy! Ohhh! It's so decadent! It's fantastic!" For weeks after, people came up to me saying, "I just had to pull over in my car to write down the recipe, it sounded soooo good!"

Vicki moved to television in 1997 with her show Vicki Gabereau on CTV. I've been a guest on her show a few times, once to prepare a Thanksgiving dinner and another time to make a gourmet meal from Kraft Dinner with chef Michael Noble and actor Jackson Davies. Now that was a real challenge! Doug and I have also been on her show cooking up a storm on behalf of a fundraising 10-K fun run for the Alzheimer's Society. There's no doubt, Doug and I are Vicki's biggest fans. She's the best! ↺

TORTILLA DE POTATAS (SPANISH OMELETTE)

In 1997, Doug and I visited the Spanish hillside towns known as "the white villages" in the Andalucia region of Spain. In 1999, we again happily returned to Spain when Doug was scheduled to speak at an international medical-summit meeting in historic Madrid. We were also celebrating our 40th wedding anniversary, and what a celebration it was. The museums, historical buildings, dozens of beautiful fountains and parks, and the royal palace were mind boggling!

The food, of course, was also a highlight as we both enjoy Spanish cuisine. Everywhere we went, the tortillas were a must-try. Each restaurant had its own version of this classic dish, served all hours of the day as an appetizer or main course. One of my favourites was filled with fresh lobster topped with a lobster sauce – oh so decadent! The recipe here is for the basic tortilla de potatas (Spanish omelette), but seafood, meats, more cheese and peppers can be added – just use your imagination. I like to serve Tomato Salsa with this version (see page 205).

INGREDIENTS
2 medium potatoes, cut in half lengthwise (or 5 small)
1 tbsp light olive oil
½ cup onions, chopped
2 cloves garlic, crushed (optional)
Salt to taste
6 extra-large eggs
1 tbsp cold water
Pepper to taste
2 to 3 tbsp Manchego or Parmesan cheese, freshly grated

METHOD
Peel and slice the potatoes as thin as possible. Heat the oil in a non-stick, 10-inch fry pan (or use two 6-inch pans). Add the potatoes, onions and garlic; sauté over medium heat until golden. Cover, reduce heat to low and cook until tender, about 10 minutes, stirring frequently to prevent sticking. Make sure the potatoes are cooked before adding the eggs. Add salt to taste. Beat eggs lightly with the flat

side of a fork, add the cold water and pour into the potato onion mixture. Stir for just a second with the flat side of a fork. Cook the omelette, lifting the eggs to let the liquid run underneath. Continue to cook until the eggs are set. Sprinkle with pepper and the cheese.

Cover pan with a large plate and hold in place with one hand. Quickly turn the pan upside down so the omelette falls onto the plate. Slide the omelette back into the pan or pans. Cook a few minutes more to lightly brown the bottom. Slide onto serving plates. Serve with Tomato Salsa (below).

PREPARATION TIME: 20 minutes

DIANE'S SECRETS

Manchego is one of Spain's most well-known cheeses. It is made from sheep's milk and may be available from specialty cheese shops. Parmesan cheese may be substituted.

TOMATO SALSA FOR TORTILLA DE POTATAS

MAKES ABOUT 1 CUP

INGREDIENTS
¾ cup fresh tomatoes, chopped
¼ cup shallots or purple onions, finely chopped
½ cup white baby corn or yellow (canned variety)
1 clove garlic, minced
1 small jalapeno pepper, seeded and finely chopped
Pinch each salt and pepper
Pinch sugar
1 tsp white wine or sherry vinegar
1 tsp water

METHOD
Blend all ingredients together well. Can be made a day ahead and refrigerated. Serve at room temperature or slightly warmed.

PREPARATION TIME: 5 minutes

WILD MUSHROOM PASTA

SERVES 2

Give me wild mushrooms in anything and I'm in heaven! For this recipe, I use two separate pans for my mushrooms – one for chopped and one for sliced. The chopped mushrooms soak into the pasta to give it the mushroom flavour, and the sliced mushrooms, leeks and a hint of soy sauce make the topping.

If you can find mushroom pasta, all the better!

INGREDIENTS
1 lb fettucine, fresh or dry
½ cup freshly grated Parmesan cheese

PAN 1
1 tbsp olive oil
1½ cups fresh assorted wild mushrooms (shiitake, oyster, portobello), coarsely chopped in a food processor
1 tbsp chicken or vegetable stock

PAN 2
1 tbsp olive oil
1 medium leek, white part only, cut into thin julienne strips
2 cups mixed whole wild mushrooms
2 tbsp mushroom soy sauce
Pepper to taste

METHOD

Cook the pasta according to package directions. While cooking, prepare the mushrooms.

In the first pan, heat the olive oil. Add the chopped mushrooms and sauté for 1 or 2 minutes until softened. Add the stock. Set aside.

In the second pan, heat olive oil. Add leeks; simmer on low a few minutes until limp. Slice the mushrooms and add them to the leeks. Simmer on low a few minutes until softened. Add the mushroom soy sauce and pepper.

Drain the pasta. Add the chopped mushrooms and toss with Parmesan cheese. Top with the sliced mushroom and leek mixture. Serve immediately. Pass more Parmesan cheese if desired.

PREPARATION TIME: 15 minutes

 DIANE'S SECRETS

Mushroom soy sauce adds a rich, interesting taste to this pasta dish.

VILLA DELIA'S RAGÙ

MAKES ABOUT 8 CUPS

Umberto Menghi and his sister Marietta were brought up with the freshest of Italian tomatoes and the best pasta, olive oil and wines in the world. And their mother's cooking could match that of any chef in Italy. This gutsy ragù sauce handed down through generations of the Menghi family says it all!

INGREDIENTS
1 stalk celery, cut into chunks
1 onion, peeled, cut into chunks
⅓ cup parsley
1 carrot, peeled, cut into chunks
2 cloves garlic
2 to 3 sage leaves
1 sprig rosemary, stalk removed
2 lb ground lean beef or veal
1 cup white or red wine
2 cups canned or fresh tomatoes, chopped
2 tbsp sugar
3 cups beef bouillon
Salt and pepper to taste

METHOD
Put celery, onion, parsley, carrot, garlic, sage and rosemary in food processor; pulse on-and-off until they are chunky.

In a large fry pan (without oil), sauté the vegetable herb mixture a few minutes. Add the beef and sauté until browned. Add the wine, tomatoes, sugar, beef bouillon and salt and pepper. Simmer on medium heat for 45 to 50 minutes, stirring frequently, until thickened. Serve with penne or other favourite pasta.

PREPARATION TIME: 20 minutes

DIANE'S SECRETS *This sauce can be cooled and refrigerated until ready to use. It also freezes well. Halve the recipe if you don't want this much.*

MARIETTA'S TUSCAN ROASTED CHICKEN

SERVES 6 TO 8

When Doug and I were visiting Umberto Menghi's Villa Delia Cooking School in Tuscany in 1996, Umberto's sister, Marietta, teased our palates with this succulent chicken dish. Her enthusiastic husband, Silvan, served it to us with pride! This is my version of her winning dish.

INGREDIENTS

3 whole roasting chickens, about 2½ lbs each
Salt and pepper to taste
6 lemons, cut in half
15 cloves garlic, peeled
3 to 6 small sage branches (1 large or 2 small per bird)
Olive oil
1 cup chicken stock
Zest of 1 lemon

METHOD

Remove the giblets and neck from the chickens. Rinse well and pat dry. Sprinkle birds inside and out with salt and pepper. Place lemon halves, 5 cloves garlic per bird, and sage leaves in cavities. Rub olive oil over the birds. Place in a large roasting pan. Add more sage leaves around the bird. Add water to the pan to about 1-inch level.

Roast at 450°F until temperature reaches 160°F to 165°F (use a meat thermometer) or until legs are soft and there are no pink juices, about 1½ hours. Add more water to the pan as needed.

Remove the chicken from the pan, reserving the juices. Squeeze the juice from the lemons in the cavities and mash the garlic; add to pan. Add 1 cup chicken stock; bring to a boil. Strain. Cut the chicken into serving pieces; pour the juices over top. Sprinkle each plate with a little lemon zest and sage leaves, if desired.

PREPARATION TIME: 30 minutes

The saying "Poultry goes with everything" is so true. For a meal that is pure delight, serve Marietta's Chicken with Vegetable Gratin (page 138).

MOROCCAN LEMON CHICKEN

This chicken dish is ideal for an informal dinner buffet. It can be prepared a day ahead and reheated when ready to serve. I had a great time experimenting with the balance of the Moroccan spices and deciding what types of olives to include.

INGREDIENTS
6 tbsp melted butter
16 threads saffron
2 whole roasting chickens, about 2 ½ to 3 lbs each
Salt and pepper
3 lemons, cut in half
¾ cup white wine
1 ½ cups chicken stock
2 tbsp light olive oil
1 cup white onions, finely chopped
3 large garlic cloves, finely chopped
2 tsp ground ginger
1 tsp Spanish sweet paprika
¼ tsp saffron threads, dissolved in ¼ cup
    chicken stock
1 cup pitted olives, sliced in half (Moroccan
    or Greek green olives)
Zest and juice of 2 lemons
2 tbsp honey
2 cups chicken stock
½ cup whole almonds or pine nuts, toasted
    (see Diane's secrets, page 91)

METHOD

Combine the melted butter and saffron threads, mincing well to blend. Rub this mixture all over the chickens. Sprinkle with salt and pepper. Stuff each cavity with 3 lemon halves. Place in roasting pan and roast at 400°F for 15 minutes. Reduce heat to 350°F and add the wine and 1½ cups chicken stock. Roast for 1½ hours more or until tender.

Meanwhile, in a fry pan, heat the oil. Sauté the onion and garlic until softened. Add the ginger, paprika, saffron, olives, lemon zest and juice, honey and 2 cups chicken stock. Reduce sauce to almost half. Keep warm at low heat.

Remove the cooked chicken from the pan, reserving all the juices (skim off the fat). Squeeze the juice from the lemons in the cavities; add to the pan juices. Combine the pan juices with the warm sauce.

Carve the chicken, pour the juices over top and sprinkle with almonds.

PREPARATION TIME: 1 hour

DIANE'S SECRETS

Preserved lemons are a classic addition to this chicken dish, but fresh lemons work just fine. Check the Mediterranean specialty shops for bottled preserved lemon. For the olives, look for Krinos, Fantis or Peloponnese at your market or in a specialty deli.

MARGARET CHISHOLM'S SEA BASS WITH TAPENADE AND TOMATO SAFFRON SAUCE

SERVES 6

Margaret Chisholm heads the catering division of Culinary Capers, one of Vancouver's leading catering companies. She is also an active member of Les Dames d'Escoffier. For one of our fundraising dinners in 1996, Margaret prepared this spectacular sea bass entrée. Serve with buttered kale and steamed new potatoes.

INGREDIENTS
⅔ cup cornmeal
Salt and pepper
6 sea bass fillets, about 5 oz each
Milk
2 tbsp olive oil
Tapenade (see Eileen's Olive Tapenade, page 177)
Tomato Saffron Sauce (see below)
Extra virgin olive oil
Crispy Green Onion Garnish (optional) (see below)

METHOD
Season the cornmeal with salt and pepper and spread on a plate. Just before serving, moisten the fish with milk and dip fillets in cornmeal, pressing to coat well. Heat the olive oil in a medium-size pan. Add the fish and cook 8 to 10 minutes over medium-high heat, turning gently to brown both sides. Fish should barely flake with a fork when done.

When the fish is cooked, spread each piece with 2 tsp Olive Tapenade. Spoon Tomato Saffron Sauce onto each dinner plate and place the fish on top. Drizzle with olive oil and garnish with Crispy Green Onion Garnish. Serve immediately.

TOMATO SAFFRON SAUCE

INGREDIENTS
3 tbsp olive oil
1 tsp garlic, finely chopped
3 tbsp shallots, finely chopped
6 ripe Roma tomatoes, chopped
½ tsp lemon zest
½ tsp orange zest
⅓ cup carrot, grated
⅓ cup tart apple, grated
Pinch saffron
⅓ cup fish stock or water
⅓ cup white wine
⅓ cup orange juice, freshly squeezed
Salt and pepper

METHOD
In a small, heavy saucepan, heat the olive oil and sauté the garlic and shallots over medium-low heat, 2 to 3 minutes. Add the tomatoes, lemon and orange zest, carrot, apple, saffron, fish stock and white wine. Simmer 20 to 25 minutes. Purée in a blender or food processor. Strain, pressing through the solids. Add the orange juice and reheat. The sauce should have the consistency of a light purée. If necessary, add a little more orange juice to thin. Season with salt and pepper to taste and keep warm.

CRISPY GREEN ONION GARNISH
Slice 2 green onions into strips, 4¾ x ⅛ inches. Fry in sunflower or peanut oil in a deep-fat fryer or a heavy pot half full of the oil, heated to 350°F until very light golden. Drain on paper towels. Serve at room temperature.

PREPARATION TIME: 1 hour, including preparation of sauce and garnish.

CHRISTIAN'S SEARED SCALLOPS WITH MADRAS CURRY SAUCE AND CORN PUDDING

S ERVES 4 TO 6

When we opened our little
47-seat café in August 1991
with a staff of 4, little did we
imagine that in 1997 we
would expand next door to a
seating capacity of 100 with
a staff of 40! In 1995
Christian Gaudreault joined
the team and today is
general manager and
partner along with my
daughter Jennifer and me.
Christian is also a fabulous
cook, and I'm sure he would
have chosen to be a chef if
he hadn't enjoyed being the
manager of a restaurant.
He worked with Umberto
Menghi for many years, and
his experience is invaluable
to our success. The combination of Jennifer's strong lead-
ership and organizational
skills, Christian's managerial
expertise and love of food
,and my own passion for
food along with my marketing and promotions back-
ground makes for a winning
team!

Christian Gaudreault, the general manager and partner of our Tomato Fresh Food Café, loves to cook at home for his wife Starllie and friends. He's a fabulous cook, and his scallops with Madras curry are proof of that talent. When they entertain, Starllie's fabulous desserts are usually showcased as the finale. Try this dish with her Almond Cake (page 220) or Rhubarb-Strawberry Galette (page 222), two of my favourites!

INGREDIENTS
2 cups milk
½ tsp salt
½ cup cornmeal
4 to 5 ears of fresh corn, or ½ cup frozen
    corn niblets, thawed
2 tbsp whipping cream
2 tbsp vegetable oil
Salt and pepper
12 large Digby scallops (approx. 1 oz per scallop)
1½ to 2 tbsp Madras curry powder, or to taste
½ tsp salt
1½ cup plain yogurt (see Diane's secrets)
1 tbsp sugar or honey
Cilantro

METHOD

In a saucepan, bring milk to a boil. Add the ½ tsp salt. Slowly whisk in the cornmeal, beating gently to avoid lumps. Stir at low heat until the mixture thickens. Add the corn and blend in the whipping cream. If too thick, add a little more milk. It should be creamy, similar to the texture of thick cream of wheat cereal. Set aside on low heat.

Heat a large non-stick fry pan over high heat. Add the oil. Lightly salt and pepper the scallops on both sides and place in the pan, leaving space in between. Sear about 2 minutes on each side, until opaque and golden brown. They should be light and springy. Reduce heat to low and keep warm.

Heat a non-stick fry pan over medium heat. Warm the curry powder to release the full flavour, about 2 to 3 minutes. Add the ½ tsp salt. Blend the yogurt and sugar; add to pan, quickly stirring just until slightly warmed. Reduce heat to low to keep warm while you assemble the serving plates.

On the centre of each plate, spoon a little of the corn pudding. Arrange three scallops on top. Drizzle a little curry sauce over top the scallops. Garnish with a sprig of fresh cilantro.

PREPARATION TIME: 35 minutes

 DIANE'S SECRETS *Do not use low-fat yogurt for this recipe; it will curdle.*

DAVID'S WHISKY MARINATED ARCTIC CHAR WITH TOMATO CHUTNEY

SERVES 4 TO 6

During the shooting of a movie with her father in Vancouver in 1999, Gwyneth Paltrow, academy-award winning actress, frequented our restaurant. One day Miss Paltrow arrived at the Tomato with a party of three. Our supervisor, Ted Ingraham, not recognizing her, looked her in the eye and asked if she had a reservation. She said she did, but the reservation had been made in a man's name. When Ted asked her what her name was, she looked puzzled, then said, "Mary?" Ted then prepared her table, returned and said, "Mary, your table is now ready." She smiled, and everyone proceeded to the table. Customers at the next booth asked Ted, "That's Gwyneth Paltrow isn't it?" Ted replied innocently, "Oh no, her name is Mary." Ted then went to our kitchen to pick up an order, and the staff asked, "So what's Gwyneth like?" Ted then realized it must be her! But she was so impressed, thinking Ted wanted to distract customers' attention from her, she left a handsome tip! And we like to think she enjoyed our food as well! &

Our head chef at the Tomato Café, David Alsop, is the master of preparing seafood! Just to watch him tackle a whole fresh fish with the skill of a surgeon is fun, but even better is the final presentation with his surprise condiments and sauces to enhance the delicate fish.

INGREDIENTS
1 ½ lb fillet of Arctic char
2 cups water
2 tbsp coarse salt
2 tbsp white sugar
1 3-inch piece cinnamon stick
1 tbsp cracked black pepper
Zest of ¼ orange
½ cup cooking molasses
½ cup whisky

METHOD

In a medium saucepan, combine all ingredients except the fish and bring to a boil. Cool. Pour over fish and marinate in the refrigerator at least 24 hours.

Remove fish from the marinade and grill on the barbecue or broil on the middle rack of your oven, 4 to 5 minutes per side or until opaque. Watch that it doesn't burn! Serve on a bed of wild rice or mashed potatoes (see Garlic Mashed Potatoes, page 26) with Tomato Chutney (below).

TOMATO CHUTNEY

INGREDIENTS
3 tbsp olive oil
1 tbsp fennel seeds
1 medium onion, diced
3 cloves garlic, minced
3 tbsp fresh ginger, peeled and finely chopped
3 to 4 dried ancho chilies, seeded and broken into
   ½-inch pieces
1 cup white wine
1 cup white wine vinegar
1 cup white sugar
2 green peppers, diced
10 to 12 red tomatoes, peeled, seeded and coarsely
chopped

METHOD

In a medium saucepan, heat the oil and sauté the fennel seeds briefly. Add the onion, garlic and ginger. Sauté until golden. Add the chilies, white wine, vinegar, sugar and peppers. Simmer until the chilies are slightly softened, about 10 minutes. It should be the consistency of jam. Add the tomatoes and bring to a boil. Return to simmer and reduce until thick, 25 to 30 minutes. Stir frequently. Cool and refrigerate. (Keeps about 1 week in the refrigerator.)

PREPARATION TIME: With chutney, 40 minutes (plus marinating time)

DIANE'S SECRETS

Arctic char is an interesting fish when it's available, but sea bass or halibut works well with this recipe too. Ancho chilies are available at Mexican specialty stores. They give a beautiful deep red colour to the chutney, add an interesting flavour and they aren't too spicy.

GRANOLA WITH SUN-DRIED SOUR CHERRIES

MAKES 23 TO 24 CUPS

We serve this granola at the Tomato Café, and our customers love it. It's a recipe that our former chef, Lisa Rowson, introduced. It couldn't be more delicious or nutritious! At the Tomato, we serve it with French vanilla yogurt and fresh seasonal fruit. Add one of our popular fruit drinks like the Susi Q (page 116) and you have a totally nourishing start to the day.

INGREDIENTS
2 cups oat bran
10 cups rolled oats (not instant)
1 ½ cups sesame seeds, toasted (see Diane's
    secrets, page 91)
2 cups sunflower seeds
1 cup honey
1 cup vegetable oil
¾ cup water
1 ½ cups coconut
2 cups raisins
1 ½ cups sun-dried sour cherries or cranberries

METHOD
Mix the oat bran, rolled oats, sesame seeds, sunflower seeds and honey with the oil and water until the liquids are evenly distributed. Bake at 275°F for 30 minutes, stirring every 10 minutes, until evenly browned and crunchy. Remove from oven and let cool. Stir in the coconut, raisins and sun-dried fruit. Store in sealed containers.

PREPARATION TIME: 40 minutes

DIANE'S SECRETS

This recipe makes tons! Its great for gifts, especially over the holiday season. Put the granola in attractive tins, tie with a big bow, and your friends will love it! The granola freezes well, so tuck some away in sealed containers or freezer bags.

MARGARET'S BANANA BREAD

MAKES 1 LOAF

Margaret Armstrong's banana bread is the best in the world, bar none! We sell tons of her famous bread at the Tomato, and I think everyone who has bought my cookbooks *Fresh Chef on the Run* and *Diane Clement at the Tomato* has made this recipe. No matter what the decade may be, banana bread is here to stay! I just had to include Margaret's recipe in this book; it's a treasure!

INGREDIENTS
2 large bananas, very ripe (almost black)
1 tsp baking soda
5 tbsp buttermilk
1⅓ cup all-purpose flour
1 tsp baking powder
½ cup soft butter
½ cup brown sugar
1 large egg
1 tsp vanilla

METHOD
In a bowl, mash together the bananas, baking soda and buttermilk and set aside. In a separate bowl, sift together the flour and baking powder; set aside. In a mixer, cream the butter with the sugar, egg and vanilla. Mix in the banana mixture and the dry ingredients, just enough to blend. Don't overmix.

Pour the mixture into a greased 8x5-inch loaf pan and bake at 350°F for 55 to 60 minutes or until a skewer inserted in the centre comes out clean. Cool and wrap well.

PREPARATION TIME: 15 minutes

 DIANE'S SECRETS *Using bananas that are almost black is the secret to making the best banana bread. They add much more banana flavour than when they are yellow and less ripe. They're easier to blend, too. This loaf is best made a day ahead, and it's wonderful toasted!*

STARLLIE'S ALMOND CAKE

SERVES 8

Les Dames d'Escoffier recognized Starllie Spilos' creative baking talents by awarding her a scholarship to further her career in baking. Starllie chose the prestigious CIA Institute in Napa Valley, California, for her baking course. She currently teaches baking at David Thompson High School in Vancouver. Her almond cake is typical of the cakes served throughout Spain and Portugal. It makes a perfect ending to Spanish Paella (page 46). Serve with summer fruits and sorbets to add a refreshing touch.

INGREDIENTS
⅓ cup butter
⅓ cup canola or other vegetable oil
¾ cup white sugar
6 oz almond paste (marzipan), crumbled
6 oz almonds, finely ground
Zest of one orange or lemon, finely chopped
5 large eggs
½ cup sifted cake flour
1 tsp baking powder
¼ cup orange liqueur or orange juice,
    freshly squeezed
Icing sugar

METHOD
Preheat the oven to 325°F. Butter, flour and line with parchment or waxed paper the bottom of a 9-inch springform pan.

In a mixer, cream the butter, oil and sugar until creamy, about 5 minutes. Add the almond paste, continuing to beat until smooth. Add ground almonds and the orange zest, blending well. Add the eggs one at a time. Blend together the flour and baking powder, then add to the batter, mixing just until blended. Don't overbeat.

Pour the batter into the pan, and bake for 40 to 45 minutes, or until a skewer inserted into the middle of the cake comes out clean. Remove from oven; drizzle the orange liqueur evenly over the cake. (Can be made a day ahead and wrapped well.) Dust with icing sugar and serve.

PREPARATION TIME: 15 minutes

DR. JACK'S DYNAMITE CHOCOLATE TORTE

SERVES 10

Jack Taunton is the co-director of the Allan McGavin Sports Medicine Centre with Doug. He is also the team physician for the Vancouver Grizzlies. He and his wife Cheryl, and daughters Kristen and Carla Jane, are family friends. Whenever they join us for dinner, I always include a new chocolate surprise for Jack. This is my latest chocolate creation, which I dedicate especially to him.

INGREDIENTS

PASTRY
5 to 6 tbsp butter, melted
2 cups Oreo cookies, finely crushed

FILLING
1 cup butter
5 oz semi-sweet chocolate
2½ cups white sugar
½ cup light cream
4 large eggs
1 egg yolk
1½ tsp vanilla

METHOD

PASTRY
In a bowl, combine melted butter and cookie crumbs. Pat into a 9-inch springform pan along the bottom and 2 inches up the sides. Bake at 350°F for 7 to 8 minutes. Cool.

FILLING
Melt butter and chocolate over very low heat. Add the sugar and cream, stirring until the sugar is dissolved and the mixture is smooth. Beat the eggs and yolk in a small bowl, then gradually add to the chocolate mixture, stirring well until smooth and thick. Add the vanilla and stir.

Pour chocolate mixture into the crust. Bake at 350°F for 45 to 50 minutes or until set. Serve warm or at room temperature with whipped cream and chocolate curls, if desired.

PREPARATION TIME: 15 minutes

From the moment we opened the Tomato Café in 1991, our homemade desserts have been a huge hit. They are simple, comfort desserts reminiscent of our mothers' and grandmothers' home baking. Cobblers, cookies, fruit pies, bread puddings, homemade ice creams and anything chocolate bring back happy memories of devouring Mom's or Grandma's special desserts. Even in the health-conscious nineties, everyone still loved to splurge once in awhile. Here are some of the star desserts that continue to satisfy the sweet tooth. ❧

STARLLIE'S RHUBARB-STRAWBERRY GALETTE

SERVES 6

Starllie is on staff at our Tomato Café, where she lends her expertise in our bakery whenever she is free from her teaching duties. She is also married to our partner and general manager, Christian Gaudreault. Christian adores desserts, and Starllie spoils him with her superb creations! Our customers are also big fans of Starllie's special desserts, especially this amazing fresh galette.

INGREDIENTS

PASTRY
1¼ cups all-purpose flour
1 tsp sugar
¼ tsp salt
½ cup unsalted butter, frozen and cut into
    ¼-inch cubes
3 to 4 tbsp ice water

FILLING
4 cups fresh rhubarb, cut into 1-inch pieces
¾ cup fresh large strawberries, quartered
5 to 6 tbsp flour
1 cup granulated sugar
2 tbsp granulated sugar
Icing sugar

METHOD

PASTRY

Place the flour, sugar and salt in a food processor fitted with a metal blade; pulse to mix. Add the cubes of frozen butter and pulse, approximately 25 seconds, just until the mixture resembles course crumbs. Add 3 tbsp water and mix about 5 seconds to blend. If the pastry mixture is too dry, add the remaining 1 tbsp water. Remove immediately and knead into a ball on a lightly floured surface. Flatten into a round disk, then roll into a 12-inch circle, about ⅛-inch thick. Chill the pastry on a baking sheet for at least ½ hour while you prepare the filling. (Can also me made the night before and refrigerated.)

FILLING

In a bowl, combine the rhubarb and strawberries. Toss in the flour and sugar, blending well. Place filling in the middle of the pastry, leaving a 3-inch margin around the edge. Carefully fold the pastry edges over to cover the edge of the fruit filling. Pleat the pastry edges by pinching. Patch any cracks in the pastry to prevent the juices from running out while baking. Brush the crust edges with ice water and sprinkle with the 2 tbsp of sugar.

Bake at 400°F for 40 to 45 minutes or until the crust is golden brown and the filling is bubbling. Cool about 20 minutes before serving. Dust edges with icing sugar just before serving.

PREPARATION TIME: 40 minutes, including chilling pastry

 DIANE'S SECRETS *Serve with vanilla ice cream; it's the royal crown to this luscious fruit dessert.*

DIANE'S POWER COOKIES

MAKES ABOUT 2½ TO 3 DOZEN

Since we opened our doors at the Tomato, we have had our faithful daily customers. Two of my favourites I call "our dancing ladies." Mollie Thackeray and Grace Rutherford are retired and are avid square dancers. They drop by after every dance class wearing the most colourful outfits you've ever seen. Their billowing skirts drape over their seats as they sip their tea and enjoy our muffins, banana bread and scones. It's a delightful sight, and they have become our expert critics on what muffin or scone is "the best"! &

I couldn't do a cookbook without including my favourite cookie recipe. These giant cookies are full of everything good for a high-energy boost. They're a popular mid-afternoon pick-me-up for our Tomato Café customers. If you crave something not too sweet, these cookies will fit the bill. They're also great on hikes and picnics!

INGREDIENTS
1 cup whole wheat flour
1 tsp baking powder
Pinch salt
¾ tbsp cinnamon
⅛ tsp powdered ginger
1½ cups raisins
1 cup walnuts, chopped
1 cup pecans, chopped
1 cup peanuts, chopped
½ cup sunflower seeds
½ cup sesame seeds
½ cup wheat germ
1 cup rolled oats (not instant)
1 cup soft butter
½ cup creamy peanut butter
1¼ cups brown sugar
2 large eggs
¼ cup milk

METHOD

Preheat oven to 350°F. Combine the flour, baking powder, salt, cinnamon and ginger in a large bowl. Add raisins and toss until coated. Add nuts, seeds, wheat germ and rolled oats; mix together.

In a mixer, cream the butter and peanut butter. Add brown sugar and beat well. Add the eggs one at a time; blend in milk. Pour over the flour mixture and stir well or mix with your hands until the dry ingredients are well moistened.

Drop by heaping spoonfuls 2½ to 3 inches apart on a foil-lined cookie sheet. Flatten the cookies slightly. Bake for 15 to 18 minutes on the second rack from the bottom until light brown and semi-firm to the touch, but not soft. Transfer cookies with metal spatula onto wire racks to cool. They will keep fresh for 2 to 3 days.

PREPARATION TIME: 20 minutes

In 1999, the Variety Club invited my daughter Jennifer and me to appear on the Show of Hearts *as hosts for a romantic cooking segment during the 22-hour fundraisng telethon, shown live from Vancouver's Queen Elizabeth Theatre. This was the first time in the history of the show that they had attempted a cooking segment. One lucky couple would be chosen to be on stage to enjoy a romantic Valentine Day's brunch prepared right in front of them.*

The chefs I hoped to attract for the event were John Bishop, of Vancouver's Bishop's, rated one of the top restaurants in North America; Sinclair Philip, co-owner of Sooke Harbour House on Vancouver Island, ranked one of the best destinations in the world; and Michael Noble, executive chef of Diva At The Met, who received the highest honour from his peers in Canada in 1999 when he was awarded Chef of the Year by the Canadian Federation of Chefs and Cooks. Much to our delight, they all accepted!

The mighty trio presented a romantic menu that was sheer magic! We weren't too sure how the television audience would respond, but as we were waving goodbye to the viewers, the organizers rushed over to us and exclaimed, "The phones were ringing off the hook with pledges." Jennifer and I, along with our celebrity chefs and special guests, were so proud to be part of that show. The pledges topped the all-time record! 🚲

MONIQUE BARBEAU'S CHOCOLATE BANANA CROISSANT BREAD PUDDING

The combination of banana and chocolate can't be beat! Monique Barbeau was the executive chef of the 3-star Fuller's restaurant in Seattle, and she has appeared on the television show *Julia Child and Friends*. Monique is from Vancouver and is a family friend. She served this bread pudding to over 800 guests at our Taste of the Nation fundraising evening in 1993. This successful event was held at the Hotel Vancouver with proceeds going to the Vancouver Food Runners, Vancouver's prepared and perishable food recovery program, and international relief agencies. Our Tomato Fresh Food Café participated as well.

INGREDIENTS
2 whole eggs
3 egg yolks
5 tbsp Dutch cocoa
1½ cups brown sugar
1 cup heavy cream
3½ cups milk
Pinch salt
1 vanilla bean, split and scraped (seeds reserved)
½ tsp nutmeg
½ tsp cinnamon
3 tbsp granulated sugar
½ cup brandy
4 bananas, sliced
3 tbsp butter
Lemon juice
4 to 5 croissants, cut into cubes
Icing sugar

METHOD
Preheat oven to 375°F. Butter bottom and sides of a 2-quart baking dish.

In a bowl, lightly beat together eggs and yolks. Add cocoa and sugar and whisk together. Combine this egg mixture with cream and milk in double boiler over medium heat. Heat until warm.

Add salt, vanilla bean, nutmeg, cinnamon, sugar and brandy. Continue cooking, stirring constantly, until liquid thickens. Remove from heat.

In a medium pan, sauté bananas in butter over medium heat until soft. Add lemon juice. Add croissant cubes and bananas to cocoa mixture and stir well. Pour into baking dish and bake in a water bath for 30 minutes. Let cool for 15 minutes.

Spoon pudding into dessert bowls. Pour Crème Anglaise (see below), whipped cream or your favourite chocolate sauce over top. Dust with powdered sugar.

PREPARATION TIME: 25 minutes

DIANE'S SECRETS

A water bath, or bain-marie, is simply made by putting the baking dish in a larger casserole or roasting pan before baking. Pour hot water into the larger pan until it reaches halfway up the baking dish. Baking in a water bath helps maintain an even temperature around the dish and is commonly used for egg dishes, including custards and soufflés.

CRÈME ANGLAISE

INGREDIENTS
5 cups milk
Vanilla bean seeds (reserved from recipe above)
⅓ cup sugar
16 egg yolks

METHOD
In a heavy-bottomed pot, scald milk and vanilla bean seeds. Set aside. In a bowl, combine sugar and egg yolks. Slowly add some of the milk and vanilla mixture to temper eggs. Pour eggs back into pan with rest of milk. Stir continuously over medium heat until mixture thickens. Remove from heat and let cool.

PREPARATION TIME: 5 minutes

JOHN BISHOP'S MAPLE SYRUP ICE CREAM

MAKES 4 CUPS

John Bishop's restaurant, Bishop's, has been voted the number one restaurant in Vancouver and British Columbia year after year. I have shared the television and radio stage with John over many years in numerous fundraising causes. When he agreed to join us for the Variety Club's Show of Hearts in 1999, he made this homemade maple syrup ice cream to serve alongside his crèpes with Grand Marnier. This recipe comes from John's latest sensational cookbook, launched in the fall of 1999, *John Bishop: Cooking At My House.*

INGREDIENTS
¾ cup maple syrup
4 egg yolks
2 cups light cream
2 cups whipping cream

METHOD

Place maple syrup in a heavy pot and simmer until it is reduced by about half. Remove from heat and cool to room temperature. In a stainless steel bowl, combine the maple syrup and the egg yolks and whisk until well blended.

In a heavy-bottomed stainless steel pot, heat the light cream. When just below a simmer, add a small amount of it to the yolk mixture to temper it. Pour mixture into pot and cook until the custard coats the back of a spoon. Remove from heat and stir in whipping cream. Let cool completely. (Can be refrigerated overnight.) Freeze in an ice cream maker according to directions.

PREPARATION TIME: 20 minutes (plus freezing time)

"So you want to open a café ... with your mother!" My mom is a miracle of energy, well-being and joy. As her daughter for over 30 years, I can say it is truly amazing just how much she accomplishes in life – and how well. Looking back, I realize that my love of theatre, acting, food and people was born out of my early years spent literally at her apron strings. And those apron strings went everywhere – from grocery stores, to restaurants, to cooking classes, to track practice and track meets, to travel around the world, to meetings, to occasions with family and friends (complete with theme menus and props). I always felt I was an important part of it all.

Zoom ahead to 1991. I was working across the country, acting professionally in the theatre, and my Mom was doing, well, a million different things. It started innocently enough, with a discussion with friends Haik Gharibians and Jamie Norris about the need for casual, comforting cafés in Vancouver. Next thing you know, we all had paint brushes in one hand and Brillo pads in the other, cleaning up our perfect find, an original 1947 neighbourhood diner. We turned it into a contemporary café with a nod to the past. Tomato was born that summer and we have never looked back.

I call my mom "Diane" at the Tomato – as business partners we wanted to create a different relationship at work. So now, for me, she is Diane at the Tomato and Mom when we are at our homes. It seems to work well. Ironically, she soon became known as Mama Tomato to everyone at the café, partly because her free-flowing advice to staff and customers alike was dished out with every special, and partly because she headed up the team making real comfort food – food your mother would cook if she had the time! Mama Tomato with her flaming red hair is really the heart of the team, good, fresh food is the game, and making people happy is the aim.

Over the last nine years the Tomato has grown, evolved and transformed. It hasn't all been easy. Learning to run a business with your mother has its challenges (telling your mother she has to stop talking to the staff for just a few moments so they can get their work done has its repercussions!), but all in all, it has been fantastic. And the key has always been that we run the business from a family perspective – with care, with love, with passion, with joy, with respect. These are the gifts my mother shares with everyone.

I know there is still a lot to learn at her apron strings.

– JENNIFER CLEMENT ᦚ

DIANE'S HELPFUL HINTS FOR
HEALTHIER COOKING

Today, more than ever, there is a focus on maintaining a balanced lifestyle, and subtle adjustments to our everyday eating habits and how we prepare our food can make a significant difference. Remember, your everyday meals should be as healthy as possible, and often drastic changes will not be needed to your current diet. Just keep the target in mind: less fat, less sugar, less salt and more complex carbohydrates (starches). Here are some simple pointers that I have incorporated into my day-to-day life and cooking techniques. Before you know it, these small changes will make a lasting difference in your whole approach to healthier eating.

1. Start each day with a good breakfast – no excuses! If time is limited, try The Fitness Group Smoothie (page 115), which will give you your jump start for the day.

2. Serve only moderate amounts of food and fewer dishes per meal, and say no to second helpings! Trim off all visible fat from meats, and remove poultry skin. Serve small portions of meats and poultry. Remember, only 12% of your daily food intake should consist of protein, which can be found in cheese, eggs, whole grains and other food besides meat and fish. Serve larger portions of vegetables, fruits and grains.

3. To keep calories down when entertaining, eliminate the appetizer course and go straight to the soup or salad. Desserts may include a special treat, but in small portions, to satisfy that sweet craving!

4. Roast, blanch or lightly sauté vegetables for best taste and appearance. When sautéing, use a non-stick pan with just a little light olive or vegetable oil, or none at all. Keep the heat on low, and the natural juices from the vegetables will keep them from sticking to the pan or burning. After your vegetables have been cooked, a good squeeze of fresh lemon juice on them will enhance their flavour (especially asparagus and broccoli) without the need for butter. I also like to add the zest of lemon or lime to freshly grated pepper to sprinkle on vegetables, meats and seafood, either before or after cooking.

5. The fabulous varieties of fresh bakery breads available today are endless. With such great breads, who needs butter? Remember, 1 tablespoon of butter equals 100 calories: that's a lot!

6. Don't hesitate to use a little wine in your cooking. Most of the alcohol (calories) evaporates in the cooking process, but the flavour remains.

7. Substitute skim milk for whole milk. Yes, you can get used to it! Once you do, whole milk will taste like whipping cream. Likewise, use low-fat yogurt.

8. Use lower-fat cheeses. Chèvre cheeses, made primarily from goat's milk, are approximately 20% butterfat, as compared to 40% for Cheddar, Brie and Camembert. Chèvre also melts to a smooth consistency perfect for pastas and other sauces – no need to add heavy creams and butter. Fresh grated Parmesan cheese, as well, is relatively low in fat content, and a little goes a long way! (Avoid tasteless tinned, pre-grated Parmesan with its additives, and buy fresh chunks of the real thing from your local cheese deli. My first choice is Parmigiano Reggiano, from Italy's Parma region, one of the finest cheeses in the world.) For best flavour, grate your own Parmesan at the last moment. Ricotta and cottage cheese are two other varieties that are low in fat. Both are perfect for lasagna-type dishes.

9. Oil, like all fat, should be used sparingly. The best oils to use in cooking are the polyunsaturated ones, such as safflower or sunflower. Use less of any oil, including olive oil, which is mono-unsaturated. Salad greens need just a little oil dressing to coat lightly, and when you are sautéing, if you use a non-stick pan, a little oil goes a long way. I usually use only one or two tablespoons of any oil, even if the recipe calls for more.

10. A little salt goes a long way! Use fresh herbs and spices to boost the flavour of food instead of salting. Dried herbs and spices will keep their flavour for about six months and then they start to deteriorate and are tasteless. Fresh herbs are always preferable and are readily available in most markets, or try growing them in your own garden! (Always use three times the amount of fresh herbs as dried.) Here is a run-down of my favourites:

Basil: I couldn't cook without it, and fresh it must be! Dried basil is totally different and lacks flavour. (For a delightful taste experience, try this unique salad combination: On a platter or on individual plates, alternately arrange tomato slices (⅓-inch thick thick) and fresh or canned mango slices (¼-inch thick). Drizzle your favourite olive oil over the salad. Sprinkle julienne strips of fresh basil over top, along with a dash of pepper. Serve.)

Cilantro: Also known as Chinese parsley and a member of the coriander family. Its flat green leaves have a distinctive aroma and taste, and should be used sparingly. It is often used in Chinese and Mexican dishes. People seem to either like its distinct taste, or hate it!

Cumin: A member of the parsley family, with a slightly bitter taste. Only the seeds, which resemble those of caraway in both looks and flavour, are used in cooking. It is a basic spice for curries and Middle Eastern cuisine, which gained popularity in the nineties.

Dill: A popular herb for most home gardeners. Its refreshing flavour adds to many seafood dishes and salads. It's one of my favourites for Maritime chowders!

Fennel: Because of its sweet licorice flavour, this vegetable is also used as an herb. It's excellent with fish and chopped in soups and salads. Both the stalks and feathery leaves are used in salads. It's also a treat to slice it thin, let it sit in ice until well chilled, then munch on it instead of celery!

Garlic: Not really an herb or a spice, but because of its intense flavour, it is usually considered to be one. Garlic is a member of the lily family, and it has long been thought to contain natural medicinal qualities. Garlic-enhanced vitamin pills are the big rage, but using fresh garlic in your cooking is the best way to go! Never use the dried version when fresh garlic is available everywhere! Be careful not to burn garlic when you sauté it, as it will taste extremely bitter. If you do burn it, even slightly, throw it out, wash the pan and start over. It's a good idea to sauté onion and garlic together, so that the onion juices will prevent the garlic from burning. And remember, always take out the green root whenever it appears in a clove of garlic. It's very hard to digest!

Rosemary: The king of the aromatic herbs! Its rich flavour enhances roasted vegetables and meats, particularly lamb. It's great for garnishing dinner plates and is at its best when fresh!

Thyme: Usually combined with marjoram for flavouring soups and vinaigrettes and is one of the herbs used in Herbes de Provence (page 196). Thyme is one herb that is acceptable when dried.

Turmeric: Comes in powdered form and is actually a root that is a member of the ginger family. It contains a bright yellow dye that gives its distinctive colour to curries and other Far Eastern dishes. It can also be used in place of saffron to give colour to food, although it has a slightly bitter taste. Use sparingly.

Fresh herbs will keep for up to a week in the fridge. Some, such as parsley and cilantro, can be treated like flowers, put into a glass of water, covered with a plastic bag and refrigerated. Others, such as basil, rosemary and thyme, should be patted dry, wrapped in paper towels and stored in plastic bags in the vegetable compartment of your refrigerator. Fresh herbs can also be chopped finely and frozen in ice cube trays. Put about 1 tablespoon in each cube, fill with water to cover and freeze. Store frozen herb cubes in plastic bags; add to soup and stews as required. The herbs might turn dark in the frozen cubes, but they will keep their fresh flavour for up to six months!

Finally, remember this one basic rule for healthy eating and cooking: if you don't have it, you can't eat it! In other words, don't keep in the house tempting munchies such as rich cakes, cookies, chocolate, ice cream, candies, high-fat cheeses, potato chips and nuts. Instead, keep on hand plenty of fresh fruits and vegetables and unbuttered popcorn for snacks. You'll be surprised how soon your family will adapt to the new style. Treat times are special times!

DOUG'S TIPS FOR HEALTHIER LIVING

Diane and I have enjoyed a life full of adventure and good fortune. From our first meeting on the 1956 Canadian Olympic team in Melbourne, Australia to our 40th wedding anniversary in Madrid, Spain in 1999, we have travelled the world experiencing exotic cultures. It has been a life focused on family, food, sports, exercise, medicine and education.

Over the last five decades, we have seen a tremendous rise in North American society's dedication to regular exercise as well as a marked move toward healthier eating. Having faced and conquered my own health challenges – heart disease in 1979 and, more recently, a stroke in 1998 – Diane and I have become even more devoted to an active lifestyle and healthy eating.

As the 21st century begins, the message on diet and nutrition is now making a real impact on our behavior. Heart disease is now declining and life expectancy is rising. Children born today have a life expectancy of over 100 years. This clearly is a result of improved lifestyle, increased exercise and better nutrition. However, extending life without health and independence is not the goal. Our view of aging is changing. Aging with a "zest for life" is the target. The following tips will help you live long, live well and, ultimately, enjoy more time with those who matter the most – family and friends.

1. EXERCISE

Regular physical activity promotes muscle maintenance, improves cardiovascular and respiratory function, increases brain perfusion, reduces susceptibility to cancer and diabetes, facilitates digestion and bowel function and boosts bone mass. Diane and I run about 40 minutes at least five times per week.

2. NUTRITION

A balanced intake of calories is necessary to achieve proper body weight for health. Leanness is associated with increased active life expectancy. Diets rich in antioxidant fresh fruits and vegetables, low in fat and sodium but high in fibre, appear to cut the risk of chronic diseases. Moderate use of alcohol, especially red wine, seems to reduce heart disease. Diane and I have 4 ounces of Dubonnet at most dinners.

3. SUPPLEMENTATION

Prudent use of supplements to augment diet is a growing trend. Aging is due in part to the oxidation generating free-radicals that effect of our body's cells. Free-radical scavenging vitamins may lower the risk of age-related diseases.

Diane and I take vitamin C, vitamin E, a multivitamin, calcium and aspirin. I also take 500 mg of magnesium and Coumadin because of my heart condition.

4. STRESS MANAGEMENT

High cortisol levels associated with chronic stress may reduce the effectiveness of the immune system and increase risk of disease. Diane and I have a life full of satisfying activities with our family and friends, and we try and match our busy schedule with regular vacations blended with our interests in food, exercise and medicine.

5. LIFESTYLE

Aging is accelerated when a person is exposed to environmental toxins. Lifestyle choice can help retard these factors. Exposure to cigarette smoke ages the skin of the face dramatically as does overexposure to the sun. Our laws on smoking in public will protect non-smokers. Diane and I have worked with the KINeSYS Pharmaceutical Company in the development of their sunscreens suitable for athletes and active exercisers. Using UVB sun blocks with an SPF of 15 is essential to limit the danger of sun exposure.

Epilogue

THEY SAY THAT AS YOU GET OLDER, TIME GOES BY QUICKER THAN EVER! AS I LOOK BACK over the past five decades, it does seem that life is made up of fleeting moments. But sharing my love of food, travel and healthy lifestyle with my family, friends and people I meet every day has given me a rich, fulfilled life.

The "fabulous fifties and sixties" introduced Doug and me to international travel, different cultures and diverse cuisines. The "gourmet seventies" was the decade of recreating those cuisines in our own kitchens, sometimes going a little overboard with too much of everything for our dinner parties! And then the "exuberant eighties" and the "explosive nineties" were the decades when everyone began to address health issues and take a fresh look at diet and exercise. Doug's heart problem was definitely our family's wake-up call! Now, in the new millennium, we are asking ourselves, what are the most important priorities for our family? What do we value the most in life? What do we wish for in the years to come?

Looking back over the past five decades, it's clear that the most important factors in life are the love of family, in whatever form that may be, health and well being. One prime ingredient that Doug and I have shared with our family over these many decades is an adventurous spirit that enables us to enjoy life to its fullest! We have accomplished our journey with gusto and love. The challenge for everyone is to welcome new adventures and to find the ideal balance. It's there for the taking for all of us. Take time to have fun, to walk a little, enjoy Sunday dinners with family and friends and to nurture one another. Life can't get any better than that – these are the "words of wisdom" from our grandparents many decades ago. In the new millennium, we have come full circle, back to the family values of our ancestors, and as we look to the past for wisdom, we look to the future with optimism!

Table of Equivalents

WEIGHTS & MEASURES

IMPERIAL	METRIC
¼ tsp	1 mL
½ tsp	2 mL
1 tsp	5 mL
1 tbsp (3 tsp)	15 mL
1 fl oz (2 tbsp)	30 mL
¼ cup (4 tbsp)	60 mL
⅓ cup	80 mL
½ cup	125 mL
⅔ cup	160 mL
¾ cup	180 mL
1 cup	250 mL
1 qt	1 L
1 oz	28 g
½ lb	227 g
¾ lb (12 oz)	340 g
1 lb	454 g
2.2 lb	1 kg
3 lb	1.4 kg
4 lb	1.8 kg
5 lb	2.2 kg

OVEN TEMPERATURES

FAHRENHEIT	CELSIUS
200	100
250	120
275	140
300	150
325	160
350	180
375	190
400	200
425	220
450	230
475	240
500	260

Index

Potatoes

    in cod cakes, 48

    in colcannon casserole, 82

    garlic mashed, 26-27

    reheating mashed, 27

    roasted with root vegetables, 196

    Romanoff, 24

    in seafood chowder, 22

    sweet (yam) and butternut squash
        purée, 140-41

    tortilla de potatas (Spanish omelette),
    204-05

    in zucchini soup, 192

    See also Vegetables and side dishes

Potatoes Romanoff, 24

Puck, Wolfgang, 113

Purées

    mango, 159

    raspberry, 107, 157

    yam and butternut squash, 140-41

Quiche Lorraine Tartlets, 72-73

    Plate # 8

Quick Cheddar Cheese Bread, 151

Quick Pasta with Clams, 146

Rice

    arborio, 113, 142

    nasi goreng, 96-97

    in paella, 46

    pilaf, 139

    See also Risotto

Richmond Kajaks, 9, 66, 96

Rijstaffel. *See* Nasi Goreng

Risotto

    mushroom, 142-43

Roasted Garlic Potatoes and Root
    Vegetables, 196

Roasted Squash Soup with Pumpkin
    Seeds, 190-91

Ruth's Nova Scotia Seafood Casserole,
    44-45

Salad(s)

    asparagus niçoise, 78-79

    BC Hot House sunpower Moroccan,
    126-27

    Caesar, 76-77

    Crab Louis, 18-19

    deluxe, 20

    with duck and crispy wontons, 182-83

    in the eighties, 125

    flaming spinach, 130-31

    fresh asparagus, 125

seared scallops with curry sauce and
corn pudding, 214-15

shrimp Indonesian, 98-99

snapper, 46

Thai prawn dip, 174-75

tuna noodle casserole, 38-39

whisky marinated Arctic char, 216-17

See also Cod; Oysters; Salmon; Sea
Bass; Shrimp

Seasonings

ancho chilies, 217

cumin, 231

garlic, 199 (roasting), 232

green peppercorns, 125, 182, 183

herbes de Provence, 196, 197

spice Parisienne, 91

turmeric, 232

Shamrock Salad, 75

Sharon's Caesar Salad, 76-77

Shimmering Orange Mandarin Jellied
Salad, 21

Shrimp

Indonesian, 98-99

(jumbo) in fondue, 50

in mushroom seafood pie, 94

in seafood casserole, 44

See also Seafood, prawns

Shrimp Indonesian, 98-99

Soups

black turtle bean, 132-33

chilled, 136-37, 187

chilled peach-mango, 187

clam or seafood chowder, 22-23

cream of tomato, 80-81

gazpacho, 136-37

roasted red pepper, 188-89

roasted squash, 190-91

sweet onion, 134-35

zucchini, 192-93

"Spa cuisine." *See* Guérard, Michel:
and "nouvelle cuisine"

Spanish

chilled soup (gazpacho), 136-37

paella, 46-47

sangria, 13

Spilos, Starllie, 220, 222

Spinach

and eggs Benny, 85

salad (flaming), 130-31

Spreads

pesto mayonnaise, 83

relish (peperonata), 122-23

sun-dried tomato chèvre, 135

Squash

with roasted garlic and sun-dried
tomatoes, 198-99

soup with pumpkin seeds, 190-91

and yam purée, 140-41

Starllie's Almond Cake, 220

Starllie's Rhubarb-Strawberry Galette,
222-23, *Plate # 31*

Steak Superb, California-Style, 40-41